The Essential Guide for New Soccer Referees

Things I Learned the Hard Way
By
John M. Wargo

For questions, comments or suggestions, please contact:

McNelly SoftWorks, LLC
P.O. Box 13037
Fairlawn, Ohio 44334
www.mcnellysoftworks.com
Phone: 330.836.8622
Electronic Mail: info@mcnellysoftworks.com

ISBN: 1-4196-8233-4
Printed in the United States of America

What people have said about this book:

"This book bridges the gap between taking the referee class and passing the test to showing up for your first game. It's a great tool to help new refs prepare mentally and physically for their first season."

Dusty Matthews
Hudson, Ohio

"This book will become mandatory reading for all new officials; that being said, referees at all levels will discover ideas to improve their game."

Thomas W. Turner, Ph.D.,
Director of Coaching and Player Development
Ohio Youth Soccer Association North

"At last, a referee book that contains sound advice and guidance to help the 'New Referee'. It's all there, everything you need to get started."

Michael Porpora
Wadsworth, Ohio

"This book is the ultimate checklist for any new referee. The details, examples, exercises and personal experiences the author includes throughout this book show his true passion and knowledge of the profession of Soccer Refereeing."

Brent Thornton
Waterloo, Ontario

Table of Contents

Introduction

This book is for new Soccer Referees. If you want to become a Soccer Referee and you don't know how to get started or if you just completed your first Referee clinic and you want to know what to do next — this book is for you!

What Now? covers everything from finding your first clinic all the way through getting ready for your first game to completing your first season. You should be able to read this book from cover to cover and learn everything you need to know to start your career. You may also come back to this guide periodically throughout your career and find new things that can help you.

Note: This book does not contain any discussion of the Laws of the Game; it is designed to be a supplement to the materials that do.

As I prepared to retire from a 23-year career of Soccer officiating, I started thinking about all of the great experiences I had during my career and how much I learned during that time. Since I spent many of my years as an official training new Referees, I know a lot about what is being taught to entry-level officials and what it is like working games at all levels. I know that when people decide to become a Soccer Referee, they often don't know how to get started.

Some of the biggest challenges for new Referees are figuring out how to get the proper equipment, how to locate local Referee Associations or how to hook up with Assignors to get games.

If you are thinking about becoming a Referee but have not yet attended your first clinic, jump ahead to the Appendix and read about the different types of Soccer Referees and how to locate your first clinic. I will wait here until you finish — C'mon back when you're done.

Credits

I would like to offer many thanks to all of the Officials, Assignors, Coaches, Players and Administrators who have helped me over my career. Very special thanks goes to my friend and mentor Rick Hanna — who made me understand early on how important professionalism is in an official's life. Rick was an amazing mentor and had a tremendous impact on the kind of Referee I became.

Special thanks to Charles Montague, a long time friend, colleague and the "Official" editor of the book.

The book's unofficial editor is my wife Anna, who helped me in every aspect of the book's creation. I thought Soccer was the true love of my life until the day I met Anna.

Thanks also to longtime friends and colleagues Michael Porpora, Tom Chapman, Dusty Matthews and Marvin Vastbinder, who added to the quality of the book by helping with a peer review of the first draft.

This book is dedicated to the memory of the helpful colleagues who passed away during my career: Rick Schlue and Frank Fiehn. Rick taught me most of what I know about how to deal with what happens when the ball bounces around among players in the Penalty Area. Frank got me many of my best games and my start as a Referee in three different Professional Soccer leagues.

The back cover photo (yup, that's me) was provided courtesy of Mike Wise.

The cover design was created by Teri Schott of Sure Schott Design.

About the Author

For John Wargo, the love of soccer started in elementary school, where he played on a team that made it to the championship series every year. It was the start of a decades-long dedication to the sport.

In the 1980's John decided to expand his soccer career to include the world of officiating. He completed the Ohio High School Athletic Association (OHSAA) Soccer Referee certification course and exam and immediately followed-up with the US Soccer Entry Level Referee Certification course and exam. This was the beginning of a 23-year career as a Soccer Referee. He worked his way up through both the USSF and OHSAA Referee ranks, eventually achieving USSF State Referee and OHSAA Class 1 Referee status.

Early on in his career, John moved into the professional ranks, working in four different Professional Soccer leagues (indoor and outdoor) and officiating many televised games — including a position as a Referee on the NPSL 1993 All Star Game. John's busy officiating schedule took him all over the United States and he worked with some of the highest level referees in Soccer — including games with more than ten FIFA Referees.

In the mid 1990's John expanded his Soccer career to include new referee instruction. John became a USSF Referee Instructor, eventually earning the status of USSF State Referee Instructor. As an instructor, John taught at all levels, focusing most of his attention on teaching the USSF Entry Level Referee Course. Because of his extensive experience in training new referees, his skill at presenting the material and his knowledge of the rules, he was asked to help with the creation of the USSF Recreational Referee and USSF Recreational Referee Instructor Course materials.

During his officiating career, John found many ways to give back to the game of Soccer — including mentoring new referees.

From his experience teaching the Entry Level and Recreational Referee courses and all of the years mentoring new Referees John discovered that most new Referees needed help bridging the gap between the first Referee clinic and the career that follows. That was the inspiration for this book.

After a full and rewarding career, John has now hung up his whistles and cards and is focusing his time on helping his wife Anna raise their beautiful 4-year-old twins. He can't wait until they take up the game and, yes, hopes that they might even become Referees some day.

Chapter 1

After the clinic

OK, you have finished your first Referee clinic and you are ready to get started. In this chapter you will learn everything you need to prepare for your first game as a Soccer Referee.

Know it All! After completing your first clinic and reading all of the materials provided to you, there should not be any aspect of the laws of the game that you don't know or understand.

The first thing you should do once you have completed the clinic is take some time to review all of the course materials you received. Read from cover to cover any rule books, study guides and Referee procedure guides.

A week later, dig out all of the materials and do it again, just to make sure you know the material as well as possible. If you are reading the rule book and you find something you did not remember from the clinic, chances are you need to read it again. Apparently you don't know the material as well as you thought you did!

Additional Learning Materials

The smart Soccer Referee is constantly on the lookout for information that can help him or her become a better Referee. While any clinic you attend should help you in your career as an official, there is no possible way you will be able to learn everything you need at the clinic.

The learning materials (books, handouts, exercises and so on) you receive during the clinic are not the only resources available to help you become a better Referee. Many Soccer and Referee organizations offer publications that can be downloaded from the Internet or purchased for a reasonable price. Additionally, many Referees (like me) have written books covering different aspect of Refereeing. There are also many web sites and mailing lists that you can access that provide all sorts of useful information.

You should begin building a collection of additional resources that can help you become a better and more knowledgeable official. Look at many of the books on sports officiating available at your local bookstore, at amazon.com or elsewhere on the web. You'll find a list of additional web resources at the end of this book (see "Appendix D — Additional Reference Material" on page 105).

Joining a Referee Association

One of the first things you should do after completing your first Referee clinic is to join a local Soccer Referee Association. These associations are usually local groups that provide support and additional educational opportunities for any Soccer Referee. The groups usually meet throughout the year and allow you to:

- Meet other Referees in your area
- Get introduced to different leagues in your area who are looking for officials
- Learn about upcoming tournaments and register your availability to work games
- Discuss game situations you faced and didn't know how to handle
- Learn about game situations other officials have faced and how they dealt with them or how the group felt the Referee should have dealt with them
- Receive formal training on yearly rule changes from the sport's governing body
- Learn about local rule changes implemented by area leagues
- Receive additional training or learn about upcoming Intermediate or Advanced Referee clinics
- Learn about opportunities to advance your Referee career

Get Connected! You are not required to join a local Referee association, but if you don't, you may be working in a vacuum and will not be able to use others to help you further your understanding of the game or help with the advancement of your career.

The most important value of the local Referee association is in what you learn from others who are doing the same thing you are doing. Even though you might think you are doing everything right, it is only from working with others that you will be able to learn about other aspects of the game you might not have been exposed to yet.

Local Referee Associations normally charge a small membership fee (to help cover their yearly operating expenses) and sometimes offer family discounts.

Another important organization you will want to know about is the National Association of Sports Officials (NASO). Sample NASO services are:

- *Sports Officials Security Program* and *Game-Fee Protection Program* insurance for officials
- *Legal Information and Consultation Program* – legal counsel for officials who require it
- Lobbying of national, state and local governments for legislation favorable to sports officials
- Yearly Referee Summit events where Referees of all sports meet and discuss issues affecting all officials

Membership in NASO also includes a subscription to a special NASO Edition of *Referee Magazine*. With membership in NASO, sports officials get additional insurance (beyond the insurance they may get from their registration with a Soccer organization) and additional services and support.

As you build your career, you should look into joining NASO. For more information about membership and member benefits visit their web site at www.naso.org.

Request a Mentor

Many State Referee organizations, State Soccer associations and even local leagues have developed Mentoring programs for new Referees. With these programs, you are assigned to one or more experienced Referees who will work with you to make sure your first season goes smoothly. Mentors will perform some or all of the following activities and more to help you become a successful Referee:

- Help you prepare for your first few games

- Attend one or more of your games for moral support and watch how you do

- Deal with parents and coaches so you don't have to during your first few games

- Invite you to one of his or her games so you can see a different side of things

- Answer any questions you have about game situations or application of the rules

Having a Mentor is a great asset when starting out. You can also establish good relationships with the better Referees that you work with. Almost all experienced referees are happy to assist new Referees by providing feedback, answering questions and giving tips. They will be happy to help if you show them that you want to learn and are teachable. You can learn things from experienced Referees that would take you many, many games to learn on your own.

If you become part of a Mentoring program, ask as many questions you can and get the Mentor as involved as possible with your career. He or she is there to help you succeed.

To find out more about the availability of a Mentoring program, contact your local league or Referee Association for more information.

Equipping Yourself

Now that you have completed your first clinic and reviewed all the training materials you have, it is time to put together your Referee Kit (equipment bag). There are certain required pieces of Referee equipment and there are some extra items you might want to keep in your bag or in the trunk of the car — just in case.

Don't worry if you can't afford to purchase everything mentioned here. You should purchase the required pieces when you start, then add more items to your kit as you find you need them. In this section I have listed everything I can think of that you may need. Whether or not you actually need any of these items, only time will tell.

Some local leagues or in-house programs provide their Referees with one or more uniform shirts at the end of the clinic or before every season begins. If your league provides you with a uniform shirt, then you may not need to purchase any additional shirts unless you want to work for other leagues that may use a different uniform.

Make your equipment selections remembering that a Referee has to act and look professional at all times. Just because you have a pair of shorts or shoes that you want to wear when you work games does not mean you should wear them. Referee shorts, for example, should be solid black with no extra stripes, strings or anything that is not part of the uniform showing. Shoes should be solid black, but there is little chance that you will be able find shoes like that. Instead, make sure the shoes are not fancy, that there are no bold colors or extravagant stripes.

Any local sports equipment store should stock some standard Referee equipment. Soccer Referee uniforms are different than the uniforms for Baseball, Basketball and American Football officials, so you will have to make sure you get the right stuff. Many Soccer specialty shops carry equipment specifically for Soccer Referees, so you will not have to worry too much about getting the wrong stuff from them.

There are also several manufacturers of Referee uniforms that sell direct or through stores or local representatives. Several of the most popular are listed below:

- www.officialsports.com
- www.lawfive.com
- www.aysostore.com
- www.kwikgoal.com

Official Sports International is the official supplier of uniforms for the United States Soccer Federation, The National Intercollegiate Soccer Officials Association, other organizations and professional leagues. It has by far the largest selection of Referee uniforms and equipment — usually of a very high quality.

While I do not want to promote a particular uniform supplier over another, it is important to understand that there will be a slight variation in color between supplier's uniforms. As you do more games, you will probably want to buy the best shirts from Official Sports so you will look more like the other Referees you will be working with.

When you go shopping for uniforms, be sure to keep in mind that you are probably going to need at least two uniform shirts, possibly more. Because most Soccer organizations support a primary Referee uniform shirt and usually one or more alternate jerseys, a new Referee is going to have purchase at least the primary uniform and probably at least one alternate color as well.

Most manufacturers offer both V-neck and buttoned uniform shirts. You will want to select the uniform style that matches your long-term needs. The V-neck shirt is the best choice when you are looking for an inexpensive uniform and if you work mostly by yourself or do mostly small-sided games. If you plan on sticking around for a while and working three-man games for older age groups then you will want to purchase the buttoned shirts since that is what most advanced Referees will be wearing.

Uniform Trick

I always wore a t-shirt under my uniform. That way, if I got salt stains, they were on my undershirt and not on my uniform. I could change my undershirt between games and not have to worry about keeping too many uniform shirts handy.

The t-shirt should always match a primary color in the shirt. Do not wear a green t-shirt, for example, unless the primary uniform color is green as well.

You will also have to decide between long-sleeve and short-sleeve uniform shirts. Until you can afford both lengths, select the sleeve length that works best for the weather conditions you will face most often. You will probably want to start with short-sleeve uniform shirts then add long-sleeve shirts later when you can. If you don't have a long-sleeve uniform and you're working on a cold day, you can always wear a long-sleeve t-shirt under your uniform to stay warm.

You should clean your shoes between games — some Referees even clean their shoes between periods.

Shoe Care - You can coat your shoes with petroleum jelly (Vaseline) before the game if you want to help keep water out of your shoes and make them much easier to clean later.

As you continue with your career, budget a portion of your earnings to use to purchase additional equipment over time. You will eventually have a complete and useful Referee Kit that will last you a very long time.

As part of your first Referee clinic, your instructors probably spent some time listing the different pieces of equipment you would need as a Referee. The following pages contain exercises designed to help you prepare your Referee Kit. Take a moment and think about all of the uniform and equipment items a Soccer Referee should have in his or her kit, then look on the next page to begin the exercises.

Exercise 1 - Referee Equipment (Part 1)

On a separate sheet of paper, make a list of every item you think a Soccer Referee should have in his or her kit. Put each item on a separate line; you will be adding to the page in the next part of the exercise.

Your list should include uniform items plus any additional items you think the Referee should have. Take the time you need to build the most complete list possible.

Turn the page to compare your list with mine.

Exercise 1 - Referee Equipment (Part 1 solution)

The following table contains the complete list of everything you could or should have in your Referee kit.

- One or more uniform shirts
- Two pairs of Referee shorts
- Two pairs of Referee socks
- Two pairs of Soccer shoes
- At least two whistles
- Wrist lanyard
- Red Card
- Yellow Card
- Pen
- Pencil
- Flipping coin
- Pocket sized notebook or pad of paper
- Two wrist watches with countdown timer
- Rule books and other reference materials
- Shoe polish
- Shoe laces
- Air Pump/needles
- Tape measure

- Plastic trash bags
- Scissors
- Vaseline
- Spray Paint
- Athletic tape or duct tape
- Hand or bath towel
- Needle and black thread
- Referee badge
- Sunscreen
- Bug repellent
- Training Vest
- Rain gear/Umbrella
- Solid white or black baseball cap
- Water, water and more water
- Snack bars or fresh fruit
- Pain reliever such as Aspirin, Ibuprofen or Acetaminophen
- Bandages (Band-Aids for example) and ointment
- Mobile phone

If you came up with something that is not on my list, good for you! You are clearly thinking beyond the norm. If you think your item should be added to my list, email it to me at suggestions@newsoccerref.org.

Minimum Required Referee Equipment

Every beginning Soccer Referee should have the minimum required equipment in his or her kit. This is my list of the Referee's minimum equipment.

- Uniform shirt (or shirts)
- Referee shorts
- Referee socks
- Soccer shoes
- Two whistles
- Wrist lanyard (for your whistles)
- Red and Yellow cards
- Pen or pencil
- Pocket sized notebook or pad of paper
- Flipping coin
- Two wrist watches with countdown timer
- Rule books and other reference materials

Do you see anything there that surprises you? Do you think there is anything missing from the list?

Exercise 1 - Referee Equipment (Part 2)

OK, now that you have seen my complete list or equipment items, go back to your sheet of paper and identify the items that were on my list but not on your list.

For every missing item you find, think about (or jot down) why you think the item is on my list. In the solution for this exercise on the next page, you will find my reasoning for each item.

Exercise 1 - Referee Equipment (Part 2 solution)

This table contains a description of every equipment item listed in Part I. Compare your explanation for each item with the contents of this table and see if you can discover anything you hadn't thought of.

Item	Purpose
One or more uniform shirts	There are two reasons you might want to carry more than one uniform shirt in your bag. 1) You might want to have a shirt to change into between games. If you are working more than one game in a day, you might have sweat stains or mud on your shirt, so you will need to change into a clean shirt before your next game. Remember, looking and acting like a professional can help alleviate some problems you encounter during a game. 2) One of the teams or one of the goalkeepers is wearing the same color shirt as you are. If the Referee shirt is yellow and one of the teams is wearing yellow, then you have a color conflict. Even though it might be the team or player's responsibility to change, they may not have something to change into. You have to be ready to change if needed.
Two pairs of Referee shorts	If you are working more than one game in a day, you might get mud or sweat stains on your shorts. You may need to have another pair of uniform shorts available for your next game.
Two pairs of Referee socks	If you are working more than one game in a day, you might get mud on your socks. You will need to have another pair available for your next game.

Item	Purpose
Two pairs of Soccer shoes	Field conditions vary depending on time of day (dew in the morning, extreme dryness during the day), as do weather conditions (rain, mud, snow). You will want to have shoes in your bag for most field conditions you will encounter. In warm climates, you may want flats for dry days and turf shoes for rainy days or dewy mornings. For colder climates, you may want turf shoes for normal fields and cleats or studs for muddy fields. Be sure to take the right kind of shoes to every game. You will look unprofessional and have difficulty staying up with play if you are slipping and sliding all over the field because you are wearing the wrong shoes. See "The Referee's Shoes" on page 25 for more information.
At least two whistles	You will want to carry at least two during the game. The primary reason is so that if your whistle fails (either breaks or doesn't work correctly), you have another one you can quickly switch to. See "More on Whistles" on page 27 for more information.
Wrist lanyard for whistles	Sometimes a player will bump into a Referee or the Referee's arm will get hit by the ball. If you don't use a wrist lanyard or something to help you hold on to your whistles, they can fly out of your hand. It is very hard to stop a game for a foul without your whistle.

Item	Purpose
Red Card	The Laws of the Game instruct the Referee to stop the game and show a Red Card to a player under certain conditions. You will need to have a Red Card in your pocket to do this.
Yellow Card	The Laws of the Game instruct the Referee to stop the game and show a Yellow Card to a player under certain conditions. You will need to have a Yellow Card in your pocket to do this.
Pen	The Referee must keep a record of the match; you will probably want to use paper and pen to do this. Be sure to keep a spare handy in case you run out of ink.
Pencil	You may want to carry a pencil so you can write reliably in the rain. Pens don't normally write on wet paper, pencils do.
Flipping coin	The rules almost always require that the Referee flip a coin to decide which team kicks off and which goals teams defend. You will need to carry a coin to do this.
Pocket size notebook or pad of paper	The Referee needs to keep a record of several things during the match; you will probably use paper and pen to do this. Many uniform suppliers also offer special pads for Soccer Referees. They consist of sheets of paper with specific fields the Referee needs to fill in.

Item	Purpose
Two wrist watches with countdown timer	The Referee is responsible for keeping the official time for the match. You will want to wear two watches to do this. The second watch is needed in case the one fails during the match or if you accidentally stop time. Watches do break sometimes and batteries do wear out after a while. See "The Referee's Wristwatch" on page 26 for more information.
Rule books and other reference materials	Keep a copy of the rule book and other reference materials in your bag just in case you need it.
Shoe polish	You should clean and polish your shoes before every match. You will look more professional if your shoes are not dusty or covered in mud.
Shoe laces	You should carry several pairs of shoelaces in your bag. You should carry a replacement pair for your Referee shoes, but you should also have some extra laces in case you need to help repair a hole in one of the nets. Additionally, every Referee should keep a 27 inch shoelace in his or her bag. A twenty-seven inch lace (pre-cut by the manufacturer) is the exact size of the standard Size 5 Soccer ball. If you think a ball might be too big or too small, just get your spare lace, wrap it around the ball and make your ruling.
Air pump/needles	Even though it is usually the responsibility of the home team to provide properly inflated balls for the match, it does not hurt to have your own pump there just in case it is needed.
Tape measure	If you decide not to keep a 27 inch shoelace in your bag, use a tape measure instead to ensure that game balls are the proper circumference.

Item	Purpose
Plastic trash bags	Having trash bags in your Referee bag is useful for several reasons. 1) If you are working a game on a rainy day, you can put the bag on the ground so you have a dry place to sit, stretch, and change your shoes. 2) You can place your Referee bag inside the bag during the game to keep its contents from getting wet. 3) After a muddy game, you can strip off your shoes and any muddy uniform items and store them in a trash bag until you can get home and clean them.
Scissors	Useful if you need to cut a thread off your uniform or help a player with equipment issues.
Vaseline	Useful to help keep your shoes clean. Coat your shoes with Vaseline on a rainy day to help repel some of the water and make it easier to clean the mud off your shoes later. On a hot day, you can place a thin layer of Vaseline on your inner thighs to keep them from chafing while you run.
Spray paint	Even though it is usually the home team's responsibility to have the field properly lined, a referee will often keep a can or two of white spray paint in his or her bag or car trunk in case it is needed to repair small errors on the field.
Athletic tape or duct tape	Even though it is usually the home team's responsibility to attach the nets to the goalposts, many Referees keep a roll of athletic tape or duct tape in their bags to help with simple net repairs or to help attach the nets to the goalposts.

Item	Purpose
Hand or bath towel	Use a hand or bath towel to wipe the sweat off your face, neck and hands after the match. Use the towel to clean rainwater off a bench or chair. Use it to clean off the ball or to clean your shoes after the game.
Needle and white or black thread	Keep a needle and (probably black) thread in your bag so you can easily fix any problems with your uniform.
Referee badge	In many forms of Soccer, the Referee wears a badge on the uniform to show that he or she is certified by some governing body.

You might also want to keep an extra badge in your bag in case you lose one or in case you work with a licensed official who has forgotten his or hers or has one in poor condition. |
| Sunscreen | On sunny days, keep exposed skin covered with the appropriate level of sunscreen at all times. |
| Bug repellent | Keep bug repellent in your bag and apply when conditions warrant. |
| Training vest | Even though it is the home team's responsibility to have a change of uniform in case of conflict and even though the Referee normally has several uniform options available, there might be some rare case when there is no option available to have different colors (field players, goalkeepers and officials).

Some Referees keep an alternate color training vest in their bags that they can give to a goalkeeper to wear in case of conflict or wear themselves if needed. Although the rules often require the Referee to wear only certain colors, it does not hurt to be prepared for that rare situation in which there are no other options. |

Item	Purpose
Rain gear/Umbrella	It is no fun to stand around in the rain checking the field or players or waiting for the game to begin. Even though you might not be able to wear any rain gear during the game (because the rain gear may not match required uniform colors), it still makes sense to wear something to keep you dry before the game begins and during half-time.
Solid white or black baseball cap	Even though some rules might prohibit a Referee from wearing a hat, it is sometimes a necessity for a Referee to keep one handy. At a minimum, you will probably need to wear a hat if you wear glasses and you are working a game on a rainy day. If you are going to wear a hat, make sure you understand how the hat you have selected fits within the requirements of the Referee's uniform. For US Soccer, for example, the hat should be solid black with no markings of any kind. For National Federation of State High School Associations (NFHS) the hat can be solid white or solid black. Don't wear a cap with a logo (baseball cap or a golf hat) while working Soccer games. Try to look as professional as possible.
Water, water and more water	Be sure to bring water to every game. Try not to make the water too cold since cold water is hard to drink sometimes. You should pre-hydrate before every game and replace the fluids you lost at half-time and after the game.
Snack bars or fresh fruit	If you are working more than one game in a day, you will want to make sure you have some healthy food in your bag to eat between games.

Item	Purpose
Pain reliever such as Aspirin, Ibuprofen or Acetaminophen	If you are working several games on the same day or if you are injured in some way, you will want to have some lightweight pain relievers in your bag, just in case. Don't under any circumstances administer any medications to any other person. Unless you are a medical professional and qualified to dispense medicine, you should keep all medications to yourself.
Band-Aids and ointment	It is always a good idea to keep some bandages and first-aid ointment in your bag in case you cut yourself or you get a blister that needs to be taken care of.
Mobile phone	You never know what is going to happen at a Soccer game. Be sure to keep your mobile phone in your bag in case you need it to: • Call an ambulance for a seriously injured player • Call the Assignor if you think one of your partners for the game has not shown up by game time • Call the Assignor to verify assignments if more than one Referee shows up to fill a position on the game • Call the police if you are assaulted by a player, coach or fan

The Referee's Shoes

What kind of shoes does the Referee need? It all depends on the types of terrain and the seasonal conditions you will be working in.

The Referee needs to have several types of shoe depending on field conditions. You won't need all of the shoes a player may have, but you will need enough shoes to cover all of the options:

- For very dry field conditions, you will be able to wear a simple pair of Indoor Soccer shoes (flats).

- For longer grass or the dewey morning grass you will want to have a pair of turf shoes; something with 30 or more nubs.

- For rainy or snowy conditions or for muddy fields, you will want to have a pair of molded cleats to wear.

Don't worry about buying all of these shoe types right away. Do pay attention though to what kind of conditions you may be working in and get the right shoes based upon that.

A good general purpose shoe to start with would be a pair of turf shoes, but you won't be able to wear those very well on a muddy field. Molded cleats can be worn under almost any condition, but they're hard to wear on very hard ground.

I would always wear flats to a game, then change to an appropriate style of shoe once I'd inspected the field and knew what conditions I would be working in.

The Referee's Wristwatch

A Referee should wear two wristwatches. You never know when the battery will die in one of them. Additionally, some countdown timers can get stopped when a ball hits the Referee's arm or if bumped by a player during play.

It is easier if both watches are the same manufacturer and model, but there is no rule that it has to be this way. It is just easier if they are the same because you can then wear them on either wrist and the buttons and functions are the same on both.

Keep Time Running! Be careful when stopping time during the game; chances are that you will forget to start it again later. That is why **FIFA** instructs Referees to always keep the time running during the game.

You don't want to keep your watch on a neck lanyard. When you are running, it will bounce up and hit you in your face. Some Referees put the watch on a neck lanyard then hold it in their hands, but this does not make much sense to me. You will need your hands during the game — keep them free.

More on Whistles

As mentioned in the previous exercise, a Referee should carry two whistles during the game. You must carry at least two whistles because you have to be able to signal if one of the whistles breaks while you are on the field.

How you select the whistles to carry is an important decision for a Referee. When selecting a whistle, you will want to pick one that is easy to blow and one that you can easily get different sounds out of during the game. See "Varying Your Tone" on page 29 for more information. Referees need to be able to impart information using different "voices" of the whistle during the game.

Whistle Tip - When selecting your first whistle, pick one that has a little ball (the pea) in it, rather than the pea-less whistles such as the Fox 40. While the Fox 40 whistle is an awesome whistle, you will need to get some experience with your Referee "voice" before you switch over to such a sophisticated whistle.

The only time I would recommend that a beginning Referee use a Fox 40 whistle is when there is a heavy wind, rain or snow on the field; these conditions can deaden the sound of the whistle and make it hard for everyone to hear.

Two of the Same

Many Referees carry two of the same whistle on a lanyard during the game. In this configuration, the Referee can blow one of the whistles all game and switch to the other if there is a problem with the first one. Carrying two of the same whistles makes a lot of sense, but you lose the ability to completely change your tone (described below) during the game.

Two Different Whistles

As you get more experience blowing the whistle, you might want to change your whistle configuration so you have two different sounding whistles on your wrist lanyard.

The primary reason for this is so that you can work most effectively when you have two games running side by side on different fields. Since it is possible that you will have the same whistle as the Referee on the other field, players on both fields might not be able to tell whether the whistle they just heard was for them or the game next door. If you have a different sounding whistle, you can easily switch and continue with no conflict.

As you become a more experienced Referee and potentially get assigned to more difficult games, you might need to be able to signal to players that your attitude has changed. You can do this through the tone of your whistle. See the sidebar "Varying Your Tone" on page 29 for more information.

Get to Know Your Whistle! Practice with your whistle before your first game.

Nothing shows a lack of confidence like a wimpy whistle. The players can tell if you are nervous or uncomfortable by how you blow the whistle. If you seem afraid of your whistle, players may figure out that they can get away with more. Practice with the whistle; learn how to coax different kinds of sounds out of it.

Varying Your Tone

For a Referee in the middle of a fast-paced game, the whistle is his or her voice. This voice tells the players when to play, when to stop playing, when the game is over and when the Referee is upset about something. In some cases, this voice is also used to tell players when a goal has been scored.

Since players are going to have to listen to the Referee's voice the entire game, it is important that they don't lose interest in it and stop listening. You have to be able to say something with the whistle. Players have to be able to tell whether the whistle was blown for something simple or something important. Don't bore the players with the same toot every time something happens.

Players and maybe even fans should be able to tell from the Referee's whistle whether the Yellow or Red Cards are about to come out.

When a Referee switches from one whistle to another type, the sound the Referee makes changes accordingly. Referees can use this to change the sound of their "voice" by using a louder whistle.

I used a louder whistle to let players know I was starting to get upset about the way the game was being played. The louder, more piercing whistle immediately let the players know that my game had changed.

Exercise 2: The Whistle

One of the most common problems facing new Referees is their fear of the whistle. Once you have selected your whistles, spend some time practicing with each of the different styles you have selected. Do this so you are used to the whistle and ready to blow it during the game.

Many young adults are not experienced with drawing attention to themselves in a crowd, but blowing a whistle in the middle of a Soccer field is exactly that.

Referees must blow the whistle loud enough that everyone on and around the field can hear them. It often takes a lot of practice to make sure you are not intimidated by the whistle and can blow it as loud as needed.

Take a moment and think about how you have heard Referees whistle in each of the different situations listed below:

- Place kick (kick-off)
- Ball out of play over the touch line
- Ball out of play over the goal line
- Simple foul
- Harder foul
- Yellow Card offense
- Red Card offense
- Restart after a stoppage
- Getting player attention
- End of the game

Some of the situations have the same sound, but you should end up with five or six different sounds you can make. These sounds are made by whistling with different strengths and durations. You should be able to blow short, medium and long bursts on the whistle; you should also be able to do everything from toots to ear crushing blasts.

Once you have the different sounds in your head, turn to the next page and read my description of the sounds. Then, you should spend some time with each of your whistle types practicing these sounds.

Exercise 2 Solution: The Whistle

For each whistle type you have, take about 10 minutes and practice the different whistle sounds described below. Practice at least 10 times for each sound you think you will need.

You don't have to blow your whistle exactly as described, but you should have several different sounds you can make with your whistle so you can speak well with your Referee "voice."

Event	Whistle Style
Place Kick	The Place kick starts the game and restarts the game after every goal or period break. Your whistle for this situation should be a sharp blast that can be heard by everyone on or near the field. It is a sound designed to let everyone know we are starting play and they had better pay attention. The whistle should make a sharp, short to medium length blast.
Ball over touch line or goal line	Since it is usually obvious to everyone when the ball crosses the sideline, a short, simple toot on the whistle should be sufficient. If players were fighting for the ball near the line, then a slightly sharper blast on the whistle should be used – just to make sure everyone hears you.
Simple foul	A player was fouled, so you are stopping play with this whistle to deal with it. Since it is a simple foul, chances are that nobody will be upset and you will not need a very hard blast on the whistle. A simple toot, loud enough that it can be heard for about 30 to 50 yards, should be fine.

Event	Whistle Style
Harder foul	With harder fouls, emotions can get involved; you have to let everyone know you saw it and you are dealing with it. The whistle should make a sharp, short to medium length blast. Keep in mind that you should also be running to the site of the foul as quickly as possible to help manage what happens next.
Yellow Card	If you are going to be giving a Yellow Card, everyone should know it is coming. You don't want any players taking matters into their own hands before you can act. Your whistle blast is hard and of a medium to long length depending on the severity of the infraction. You should be running to the site of the foul as quickly as possible to help manage what happens next.
Red Card	If you are going to be giving a Red Card, you have a serious problem and everyone should know you are dealing with it. You don't want any players taking matters into their own hands before you can act. Your whistle blast should be hard, sharp and long enough to get everyone's attention. You should also immediately start running to the site of the foul as you blow the whistle.

Event	Whistle Style
Restart	Your whistle for a restart after a foul will vary depending on the situation. In many cases, you may not even need a whistle, a simple "Play" should be sufficient.
	For simple fouls where you have held up the game for a short period, a simple toot should be sufficient.
	For restarts near the Penalty Area, where it is possible for a goal to be scored, or for restarts after a long delay, you will want to use a sharper blast on the whistle to make sure everyone knows you're starting the game again.
Player attention	Sometimes you want to get a player's attention, but you don't want to make him or her think you are calling a foul. In this case, the whistle sound is a simple toot-toot.
	You can even extend this to a three-toot or four-toot whistle if you are trying to get the attention of someone who does not seem to be paying attention.
End of the Game	To signal the end of a game, some Referees usually blow three loud toots on the whistle, while others blow a long medium strength blast.

Get comfortable with what you think you will need to use the whistle for, then practice with each of your whistles until you are comfortable with what you are doing.

Chapter 2

Getting games

Now that you have received training and equipped yourself, it is time to set about getting some games to work.

Be Proactive! It is nobody else's responsibility to get games for you; it is up to you to get all of the games you work.

Determining What Level to Start With

The first thing you have to do is determine the level at which you will begin officiating. Depending on your certification level (Recreational Referee, Entry-Level Referee and so on, see "Appendix B — Referee Classifications" on page 97 for a description of each type), you may be restricted as to the level of games you may officiate.

Be Wise! Whether you are an adult or a young adult, you should still start out with the lowest level games available to you.

If you are not an adult (in this case, it means younger than 21), you should pay special attention to what age levels you will be officiating. There should be restrictions in place that keep you from working games played by anyone your age or older. You should make sure you don't take games in which the participants are older than you are until you get enough experience to deal with that type of game properly.

Until you have a lot of experience as a Referee and until you reach 21, you should not work as a Referee (the Center Official, the Referee in charge) for any games played by players who are older than you are. It is very important to gain players' respect and if you are younger than they are, it will be much harder to do that.

Being an Assistant Referee in games with players older than you may be difficult, but as long as the center Referee has control, you should be fine.

For at least the first few games that you officiate, select games at the lowest level for the league you are working. Use the time on the lower games to get comfortable with your new career and hone the skills you learned in the clinic. Don't jump in and do games over your head - take it easy and start slow. You will have a longer and happier career if you start easy and get comfortable before you advance to higher-level games.

Reaching out to Assignors

Even though the clinic organizers may notify local leagues of any new Referees in the area, don't sit around after the clinic complaining that nobody has called to give you games. It is likely that Assignors don't know you have completed the clinic and, even if they did, there is no way for them to know what dates and times you are available until they speak with you.

Ask your local Referee association for a list of local Assignors or a list of local leagues or tournaments. Contact every league or tournament sponsor in your area and ask for a list of Assignors. Once you have the list, select a few leagues or tournaments that have games at the level at which you want to start officiating and start contacting the Assignors.

Keep in mind that these Assignors are often very busy people and will not always get back to you very quickly.

Try by calling them first. If you reach an Assignor by phone, introduce yourself and let him or her know you recently completed your clinic. Explain how old you are, how long you have played the game of Soccer (if applicable) and how far you are able to travel to work games. Explain that you want to start easy and get comfortable with the job before you jump into higher-level games. Provide your phone numbers and the appropriate times to call you. You should also provide an email address for assignments to be sent you. Offer to send a follow-up email with your information, if the Assignor wants that.

If you are unable to speak to an assigner by phone, leave a message and be sure to immediately follow up with an email if possible. Most Assignors have families and everyone is busy, so you can never be sure the Assignor will get the message in a timely manner. In your follow-up email, list your personal information (described above) and say that you will follow-up if you don't hear back in a few days.

Many leagues or Assignors may require that you register with an assigning web site to be able to pick up games. Be sure to ask if there is a web site you can access to locate available games.

Many Assignors require referees to fill out an Availability Form that lists available dates/times, team conflicts, travel limitations and so on. Be sure to ask the Assignor if he or she would like you to fill out an availability form. They should be able to email you the form or give you an Internet URL where the form is available online.

 Paperwork Matters! Many Assignors require referees to fill out Availability Forms or register with schedule web sites before they can get games. Be sure to find out if this will make it easier for you to get games.

Rare is the Assignor that has more officials than he or she can use. For that reason, be persistent but not annoying. Just because you spoke with the Assignor, left a voice mail message or sent an email does not mean you will get games from them. Wait a few days and try again. Send an email or call and indicate that you are just trying to confirm that your information was received and you are still available.

Assignors often get last minute cancellations. If you call the night before and you have an available time slot, you can usually pick up a game.

Volunteer to work in-house program games and offer your available dates and times to anyone who you think might have games for you.

Once you have promoted yourself within the Soccer community and the Assignors know you, you will start to receive games regularly. Until then, it is all up to you.

Dealing with Pressure from Assignors

When you are discussing game assignments with Assignors, don't let them pressure you into accepting games at a higher level than you are willing to accept. In many instances, the Assignor may be desperate to get the game covered and will say something like "Don't worry, it will be an easy game" or "Don't worry, you'll be able to handle it." You are just starting out as an official and there is no possible way for you to understand what an easy game (or a hard game for that matter) will look or feel like. Remind the Assignor that you have only just started and don't want to get in over your head.

Let the Assignor know that once you have gotten a few games under your belt, you will consider doing games at a higher level. Tell him or her that you want to be doing games for a long time and don't want to burn out doing a game that exceeds your skill level. Don't worry, there are many games available and it should be easy to get more games suited to your skill level.

Assignors want Referees they can rely upon and they don't want to scare you away, so don't worry about turning down a higher assignment when you start. *Be polite and ask for an entry-level game only.*

Be Reliable

If you are going to ask an Assignor for games, you have to be willing to commit to the Assignor that you will do the game you accepted. Don't take the game as a place-holder, keeping it there until you get a better assignment. Understand that Assignors, leagues and Referee Associations expect that if you accept an assignment, you will be doing the game.

Take your commitments seriously! If you are not sure you can do the game, don't accept the assignment.

If you are holding out for a better assignment, then don't take this assignment. If you think you would rather be heading off to an amusement part or a pool party that afternoon, don't take the assignment. If you think your friends might want to do something that afternoon, don't take the assignment.

There is no easier way to get on an Assignor's "*Do Not Call*" list than to take an assignment and not show up or to take the assignment, only to turn it back at the last minute.

Do not, for any reason, take an assignment, then give it back later because you got a better assignment from someone else. If the Assignor wants to pull you off a game in order to give you a better game, that is OK.

As a Referee, you must act in a professional manner at all times; one sign of professionalism is to fulfill your commitments. Some leagues or Assignors will fine you if you accept a game, then don't show up or turn the game back later.

Accepting Your First Game

When you accept your first assignment, be sure that the game is at least a few days away. You will want to be sure that you take the time to get ready for the game. You will find specific steps to follow that will help you prepare for your first game in later sections of this book.

Don't take a game unless you are absolutely sure you can do the game.

Limit Yourself

Until you get a few games under your belt, limit yourself to one game per day. Don't rush into this. Take your time and do it right. You need time to get accustomed to being a Referee. If you are going to do two games in a day, don't accept games back to back. Make sure you have at least an hour between games so you can relax, think and prepare for the next game.

For your first few games, take extra time to prepare. After each game, take some time to analyze your performance to understand what went well and what did not go so well. You need time to digest what went wrong and to identify what you could have done differently to make the game better. You need time to reflect and learn to make sure that mistakes you made in the game are not repeated.

If something happens in the game that you are not sure how to handle, you will need some extra time after the game to research what the best response or action should have been.

If you schedule back-to-back games the first couple of days that you work as an official, the games will all blend together in your mind and it may be more difficult to learn from your mistakes. *Take your time getting started, I promise that it will be worth the effort.*

Deciding When to Advance

After you have worked from 10 to 15 games, and you feel you are doing well, you can start thinking about picking up one or two games at the next higher level.

If you had many problems in your first set of games and you were often not sure what you should have done in certain situations, you need to study the rule book and your course materials and do more games at the same level before even thinking about moving up.

Don't rush things! There is really no hurry to advance to the next level of games. You should have a long officiating career in front of you; the pace at which you move up will affect how long you remain as a Referee. If you hurry and take games at a higher level too quickly, you run the risk of getting burned out and quitting before you truly understand how to be a successful Soccer Referee. Working games at a higher level than you are ready to work is stressful and diminishes the enjoyment you will get from being a Soccer Referee.

If you have a Mentor, ask him or her for help in deciding when to advance.

Take your time, enjoy yourself — make it worth the effort and have a long career.

Chapter 3

Getting ready for your first game

So, you have put together your Referee kit, purchased your uniforms, contacted some Assignors and picked up your first game. It is time to start preparing for that game. Again, if possible you should make sure you have at least a couple of days between accepting the assignment and the date of the game; you will want to give yourself enough time to be well prepared.

Before we begin with the preparation steps, it is necessary to point out a couple of things about your first game:

- Accept that you will be very nervous for your first few games (actually, you will probably be scared to death). It is important to understand this and have reasonable expectations. Expect to be nervous, then do whatever you can to reduce your nervousness. The more prepared you are, the less nervous you will be!

- *You are going to make mistakes in your game.* Face it, even experienced officials make mistakes. Know that you are going to make mistakes. Do what it takes to minimize the number of mistakes you make. Only proper preparation and attention to detail can reduce the number of mistakes you make.

Be sure to allocate enough time to prepare for the game and you will be OK.

Pre-game Review

The night before your first game (or the morning of the game — only if you have enough time to do it well), read all of the clinic materials again. If you have the *FIFA Questions and Answers to the Laws of the Game,* have someone quiz you by asking questions randomly from the book. Get with a fellow Referee and take turns looking through the course materials or the rule book and ask each other questions on interesting topics you come across.

During your review, don't forget that some Soccer organizations (US Soccer for example) allow local leagues to modify certain rules (field dimensions, ball size and so on) to accommodate the needs of very young and very old players.

 Be sure you know about any local rule modifications in effect for any game you have accepted.

The reason all this studying is so important is that you have to know all of the material as well as you possibly can. If you know it well, then during the game, when so much is going on (players playing, ball bouncing around, coaches and fans yelling), you will be able to know what you are supposed to do without even thinking about it. If you have to take a moment to *think* about what you should be doing, you will not be paying attention to what is going on around you during that moment and you may have problems.

Stopping to think about how you should handle something that just happened may cause you to miss the next thing that happens. If the second thing is worse than the first thing, you will probably have some people angry with you, and the game will start to go downhill from there.

In a fast-paced Soccer game, you can't afford to take your attention away from the game to decide how to act. You have to know what to do in almost every situation and act quickly. Hesitation or distraction will cause problems for any sports official.

Referee vs. Assistant Referee

Trick question: When preparing to work a game as a Referee or an Assistant Referee, do you prepare any differently?

This is an advanced topic, but I thought it would be fun to include here.

Your first reaction is to say that you would prepare differently for the Referee position than you would for the Assistant Referee position. In reality though, the preparation for either position is about the same. Here's why:

When preparing for the Referee position, you have to know all of the Referee's responsibilities, actions, signals and positions. You also have to know all of the Assistant Referee's responsibilities, actions, signals and positions because you are responsible for making sure your assistants understand what you want them to do during the game. You can't tell them what you want them to do if you don't know what they're supposed to do.

From the Assistant Referee's standpoint, you will have to prepare for the game by studying all of the responsibilities, actions, signals and positions for the Assistant Referee. You will also have to do the same preparation for the Referee position because you will have to be prepared to jump into the Referee position if the Referee doesn't show up for the game or gets injured during the game and needs you to fill in for him or her in order to finish the game.

Practice

There are physical things you will need to practice before you go to your first game. Being a Referee includes brand new physical activities. You will need to make sure you know how to do them correctly and that you are comfortable doing them before you go out to do your first game.

Practice with your Whistle

Use "Exercise 2: The Whistle" on page 30 to help you get comfortable with your whistle. You don't want to be blowing your whistle for the first time at the start of your first game.

Practice Introducing Yourself to the Coaches

No, I am not kidding. Grab someone and practice how you will introduce yourself to the coach before the game. Be sure to also practice the handshake. You want to appear confident when you meet the coaches.

See "Introductions" on page 56 for more information on this topic.

Practice your Signals

Referees are required to use certain (and only those) signals during the game. It is important that players are not confused by what your signals are trying to tell them.

When you give your signals, there are a couple of simple rules you should follow:

• Don't point across your body with your arm. If you are going to point to your left and signal a Direct Free Kick, don't use your right arm to do it.

• Most signals (there's only one exception to this that I can think of — do you know what it is?) are made with only one arm. If you need to point in one direction to signal the direction of a kick and also indicate that the kick is an Indirect Free Kick, signal direction first, then switch and signal the Indirect Free Kick. Do not do both signals at the same time.

• Don't hold your signals too long, you're going to be tired enough from running. Hold them long enough to make sure that most people have seen it then drop your arm (unless you're signaling an Indirect Free Kick and you have to hold it up until certain conditions are met).

practice Makes Perfect! When you are sure you have it right, grab someone else to help you study. Give him or her the list of signals and have them randomly call out a signal for you to give. You will know you are ready when you can give every signal accurately without hesitation.

Pull out your course materials and spend some time practicing the signals you have been given. At a minimum, you should practice the signals for each of the following:

• Goal

• Goal Kick

• Corner Kick

• Throw In

• Direct Free Kick

• Indirect Free Kick

• Yellow or Red Card

Practice Patrolling the field

I know that this will look silly, so you will probably want to do this when no one else is around.

The Referee has to keep up with play, but also stay out of the way of the players — especially the player with the ball. You should have received instruction in your clinic on how a Referee should patrol the field. Read your materials on Referee positioning and go out to a field somewhere or set up a dummy field in your backyard and practice how you should be patrolling the field during the game.

Picture in your mind the following things that happen during the game and practice how you will position yourself during the game to deal with them.

- Place kick (kick-off)
- Corner kick
- Goal kick
- Penalty kick
- Goalkeeper punt

- Throw-in
- Quick change of possession
- Shot on goal and an immediate counter-attack by the opponents

If you are not sure how you should patrol the field, take a look at the section at the back of the *USSF Laws of the Game* that deals with the "Diagonal System of Control."

The Weather

Check the weather report for the time of your game; you want to be sure you pack properly for whatever field conditions and temperatures you will encounter during your game.

If it might be colder than expected, take along an extra layer of clothing (an extra long sleeve shirt, for example) that you can just throw on under your uniform. If you dress for colder weather using multiple layers of clothing, you can easily pull one or more layers off as you get warmer from running or when the temperature rises.

If there is a chance of rain, be sure to pack an umbrella or at least the appropriate rain gear you will need. Of course, you can't carry the umbrella on the field during the game, but you can at least use it to keep you dry while you prepare, at half-time and after the game.

Be sure to also take along some large, plastic trash bags. If it rains, you will be able to keep your Referee kit in one of the bags and use a second one to carry your dirty shoes and uniform so you don't get the car dirty.

How Weather Effects the Game

As you progress through your career it will be important for you to understand how the weather effects the game of Soccer.

Rain is a great equalizer in the game of Soccer. When two teams with a great difference in skills play in the rain, field conditions and the water will act to equalize the abilities of both teams. What would be a one-sided game on a dry field could become a close game on a muddy field.

Rain or snow will slow down a fast game. A wet or muddy field will take away much of the skillful play a team is capable of showing. A great player who can dance and jiggle away from the opponents with the ball, might find that he or she can barely keep control of the ball when there's standing water on the field.

Severe or continuous weather can quickly turn a safe field into an unsafe field. Standing water and large patches of mud, while fun to play in, can be dangerous for players of any age. In fast-paced games, players may be unable to control themselves when fighting for the ball. A player who can easily avoid a tackle or one who can jump sideways to avoid hurting another player may not be able to do so when the field is slippery.

The Referee must take the field condition and the weather into account when calling the game. Just because a player slips or falls while fighting for the ball against an opponent doesn't always mean that a foul has been committed. The Referee has to pay extra special attention to player contact in order to ensure that an opponent doesn't get called for a foul when the player merely slipped and fell because of the field conditions.

The Referee must also pay close attention to the field conditions and suspend or terminate the game if the condition of the field could cause the players to play in a dangerous manner.

Keeping a Record of the Game

As you prepare for the game, take a moment and think about the different things you are going to have to record (write down) during the game.

At a minimum you'll want to keep track of:

- Date and Time
- Field
- Division
- Home team name and uniform color
- Visiting team name and uniform color

- Team with kick-off
- Position of teams (which goal defended at kick-off)
- Goals
- Yellow Cards
- Red Cards

For goals, you will have to track which team scored which goals, but it might make sense to also track the uniform number of the player who scored the goal. In some cases, you will also want to track what time in the period the goal was scored.

If you give Yellow and Red Cards, you need to keep track of the team the card was given to, the name and number of the player who received it and the reason the card was given. You may also want to track the period and the time in the period that the card was issued.

If you have a serious injury during the game, you should make note of the team and uniform number of the player who was injured. You may also want to record the time the game was stopped for the injury and the duration of the stoppage.

Chapter 4

Here we are — you have your equipment, you've gotten an assignment and you were up all night preparing for the game. You probably think you're all ready to go, but there are still a few more things you need to do for your first game.

- Take a family member or a friend with you to the game. He or she can help keep you calm when you get nervous, watch your equipment during the game and help you understand how you looked or acted during the game.

- Eat a good meal, preferably one with all of the major food groups, more than an hour before the game. Food gives you energy; you will need it if you work hard during the game.

- Check the weather and make sure you are prepared for the different weather conditions you may encounter during the game.

- Take a big container of water to the game. Don't put a bunch of ice in it; fill it with whatever you get from the tap or whatever comes out of the refrigerator. The water does not need to be very cold; you don't want it to cool you down as much as you want it to replenish any fluids you lose during the game.

- Do not drink sugared drinks before the game; you don't need them. Juices and colas might taste great, but they don't do much for the athlete's overall performance.

- Plan to get there early. If you have never been to the field before, you might need extra time to find the field; you don't want to be late because you got lost. Many leagues have rules requiring that Referees arrive at the game at least 30 minutes before every game. Plan to be at the field even earlier, at least 15 minutes before the minimum time. Since this is your first game, you will need the extra time just to make sure you get everything done before the game starts.

- Practice blowing your whistles (use the exercise on page 30 as a refresher).
- Comb your hair, tuck your shirt in and pull your socks up.

Be organized and have everything ready the night before so you are not rushing around at the last minute. Getting everything ready in advance will allow you to be more relaxed as you approach your first game.

Getting There

When you get to the game, there are a few things you might want to think about.

If you arrive in a car, see if you can:

- Park in a location that is not near to either team; try to park somewhere convenient but also separate from everyone else. You don't want to be mixed up with a crowd of unhappy players when you are trying to make a quiet exit from the field. Some facilities have special parking for officials — see if you can park there.
- Back your car into the parking spot. If it is a busy parking lot, it is easier to pull forward into traffic rather than to back your way out.

At the field:

- Do not put your gear near either players' bench area. You should be able to put your stuff near the middle of the field between both benches or find some convenient place that does not get your stuff mixed up with player equipment. It is not fun when someone walks away with your bag thinking it is his or hers. Just because you have your name on your bag does not mean someone will even notice.

Presenting Yourself

People will judge you on your appearance — there is no way to get around this.

Dress for Success! A good first impression is very important and you only get one chance to make that first impression.

One of the first things I learned when I started officiating is that Referees should not look like players. As mentioned earlier, Referees should strive to look and act professionally at all times. This means that you should not dress like a player and should groom yourself as if you were preparing for a job interview. Here are some pointers to keep in mind:

- Your hair should be washed and combed or brushed.

- If you have long hair, it should be pulled back into a pony tail or controlled so that it does not flop around your face while you are running.

- If you can grow a beard, you should shave the morning before any game.

- Your shirt should be clean (no dirt or sweat stains), not wrinkled and tucked in at all times.

- Your shorts should be tied and the string should not be showing (if it is showing, it should be black so it is not easily visible).

- If you are not going to wear your uniform shirt to the game, at least wear a simple, professional-looking shirt rather than an old concert t-shirt or a shirt you wear when you mow the lawn every week.

- Your shoes should be clean, polished and tied (laces should not be frayed or knotted). Use a scrub brush to get any old mud or gunk out of the grooves and cleats.

- Your Referee socks should be on and pulled up to just below the knee.

Again, you only get one chance to make a first impression. The coaches, players and fans should sense immediately whether you are capable, prepared and ready to go. If you show up looking like a slob, look disorganized or seem unprepared, people will notice and will think they are going to have trouble with you.

The Referee who arrives at the field dressed, neat and prepared instills confidence and will get more breaks from coaches, players and fans when mistakes happen. When a disorganized or unprofessional Referee makes a mistake, the coaches, players and fans will already be expecting it and will start complaining more quickly.

Self Control Matters! Be polite to everyone - even if they have never been polite to you.

When you introduce yourself to the coaches or when you speak to any player or fan, be sure to:

- Stand up straight and tall with your shoulders back.

- Make eye contact with the person with whom you are speaking.

- When shaking hands, be sure to use a firm grip and fully clasp the hand. Your handshake says a lot about you, so be sure to act confident when you do it. For more information on how to properly perform a handshake, see *Handling the Handshake* at dummies.com (www.dummies.com/wileycda/dummiesarticle/id-704.html).

- Enforce a comfortable distance between you and the coach. If he or she steps too close, either gently put out your hand (without making contact) to help enforce your personal space or step back to give yourself more distance. If you have to, politely ask for a little more space if you need it.

- Be polite to everyone.

- Do not show anger — ever!

- Do not try to make jokes or be too friendly; you are not there to be a comedian or to be anybody's buddy.

- Do not concern yourself with anything that is not your responsibility. It does not matter what happened in the parking lot or even what happened on the field next to yours. Be focused and deal with the things you are supposed to be dealing with, nothing more.

The way you present and handle yourself makes an enormous difference in dealing with players, coaches and fans.

Before the Game

OK, you are at the field and you are ready to get started. The following tasks need to be performed before the game starts. These tasks can be done in any order; all that matters is that each one of them is covered.

If you are the Center Referee working as part of a three-man team or a Referee working the game by yourself, you will be responsible for these tasks.

If you are an Assistant Referee, you will be working with other officials and you should follow the lead of the Referee in charge of the game.

Introductions

If you are working the game as part of a team of officials, try to locate the other members of your team. As soon as you can identify them, meet and introduce yourself. Once you have your team together, it is easy to divide tasks and get to work.

Try to identify those involved in the game, including the home team and the visiting team. Once you have identified the teams, try to identify the coaches for each team.

Take a moment to introduce yourself to each coach. Be sure to follow the instructions provided earlier regarding how to present yourself to others.

When meeting with the coaches, you don't want to say too much. Say only what is necessary and:

- Don't lecture them about what you expect during the game.

- Don't identify specific things you are going to focus on during the game; they should know the rules and should know what to expect from you.

- Don't mention that this is your first game, there is no need to give them ammunition they can use against you later.

While you have the coaches' attention, take a minute to make sure you are all on the same page concerning what is going to happen. If possible, meet with both of them at the same time so you don't have to repeat yourself and the coaches from both teams hear the same thing from you.

It is sometimes a good idea to confirm with coaches any assumptions you have about the game. For example, you may want to confirm one or more of the following items:

- The age group or play level for the players
- Number and duration of periods
- Substitution procedures
- Any special restrictions on players
- Any special rules for the particular competition or league
- Tie breaking procedures if necessary
- Other topics as needed

If one of the coaches asks you a question you don't know the answer to, don't be afraid to pull out the rule book. Tell the coach that you don't know the answer to that question but you will look into it and get back to him with an answer. When you get a chance, pull out the rule book and lookup the answer. It is better to be a little nervous about having to pull out the rule book than guessing on the answer and being wrong.

Know Someone?

If you happen to know any of the players, parents or coaches at the game, you will want to be careful how chummy you are with them. Remember that you are expected to be a professional, so don't give anyone reason to think you are too close to either one of the teams.

Acknowledge the person you know, smile and say hello when you see them, but keep personal talk to a minimum. If he or she wants to talk more than you are comfortable with, suggest that you'll call them after you get home or at some later time.

Inspecting the Field

As soon as you arrive, you should inspect the field to determine whether there any issues that must be addressed. Do this early, so the home team can have as much time as possible to repair any problems you find.

Check the field to make sure that:

- All of the field lines are drawn correctly and are of the correct length. Make sure the lines are easily visible and straight.

- All field equipment is correct (goal posts, corner flags) and properly placed.

- There is nothing on or around the field that can injure anyone (dangerous items such as glass, rocks, pipes, tree roots).

- There are no large pools of standing water or huge mud puddles on the field.

- Overhanging trees or other items that might interfere with the game.

Make sure you know what the dimensions of the field lines are supposed to be before you go to the game. You won't be able to make sure the lines are of the correct length if you don't know what that length is supposed to be.

Start thinking about the types of things you would look for. From the Referee clinic you attended, you should have information on what types of issues to look for and how to inspect the field. Following this section is an exercise that will help you prepare for the field inspection. In the exercise, you will list all of the field items you will be looking for during your inspection and map out how you will perform the inspection.

When you find a simple problem with the field, fix it yourself if you can. Otherwise, tell the home coach about the problem and be sure to give the team enough time to fix the problem.

For any problem you find, decide whether the problem is critical enough that you won't allow the game to proceed until it's fixed. If it's something simple and wouldn't cause a safety problem or wouldn't effect the game, you might be able to start the game without the problem being fixed. Chances are, however, that it you've found a problem and you've brought it to the attention of the Home team coach, then you probably don't want to start the game until the problem is fixed.

Exercise 3: Field Inspection

Let's see what you can remember from your training. On a separate sheet of paper, make a list of things a Referee should look for when inspecting a Soccer field before a game. Your list should have each of the field lines plus any additional items you think the Referee should be on the lookout for. Take the time you need to build as complete a list as possible. I'll wait here until you're done...

Now that you have the list of things you are supposed to be inspecting, take a moment and look at the figure below. Map out with a pencil what path you would take around/across the field in order to perform a thorough inspection.

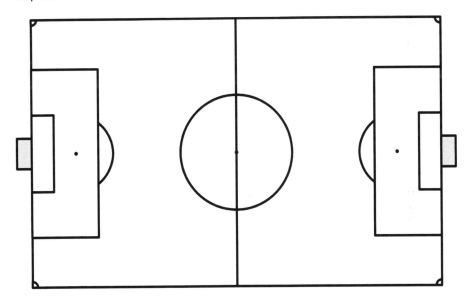

When you are finished with the exercise, you may want to take this information with you to the game; make it into a checklist or reference card and use it before every game to make sure you don't forget anything.

Exercise 3 Solution: Field Inspection

It does not matter where you start on the field for your inspection - just cover everything as efficiently as possible. The diagram on this page illustrates the route I used to inspect the field; each numbered item identifies, in order, a specific place I stopped to inspect something or to begin or end a measurement.

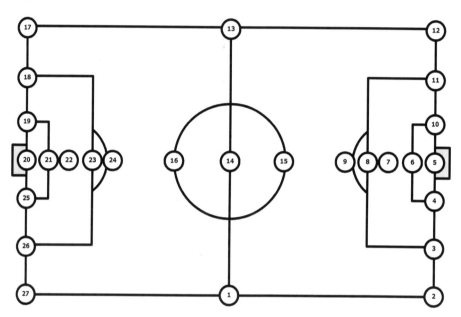

While performing an inspection of these locations on the field, the Referee or team of Referees should scan all other parts of the field looking for areas on or near the field that are unusual or could be considered dangerous for players.

The following table lists each of the inspection points and what a Referee should look for or measure at each of these points.

Step	Description
1	Start at the halfway line on one side of the field. Make sure the sidelines are visible and solid down both halves of the field. If there is a flag placed at midfield, make sure the flag is the appropriate minimum height and at least the minimum distance from the line. Turn right and head toward the corner flag.
2	Check to make sure there is a corner flag (some leagues allow for a corner cone instead), it is properly placed and is the correct (at least minimum) length. Make sure the corner arc is drawn correctly, is visible and is the correct distance from the flag. Walk toward the edge of the Penalty Area.
3	At the edge of the Penalty Area, make sure all of the lines you can see are drawn correctly and are visible. Walk toward the edge of the Goal Area and measure the distance between the side edge of the Penalty Area and the Goal Area.
4	At the edge of the Goal Area, make sure all of the lines you can see are drawn correctly and are visible. Walk toward the goalposts and measure the distance between the side edge of Goal Area and the nearest goalpost.

Step	Description
5	Verify that the goal line is visible, straight and properly drawn.
	Check the width and height of the goal.
	Check the color and width of the goalposts.
	Make sure there is a crossbar and that it is firmly attached to the posts.
	Make sure the net is firmly attached to all sides of the goalpost and the ground behind the goal.
	If the goal is portable (removable), make sure the goalpost is anchored firmly to the ground.
	Walk toward the front edge of the Goal Area and measure the distance between the Goal Line and the edge of the Goal Area.
6	At the front edge of the Goal Area make sure that all of the lines you can see are drawn correctly and are visible.
	Walk toward the Penalty Mark and measure the distance from the top of the Goal Area to the Penalty Mark.
7	Make sure that the Penalty Mark is clearly marked and the appropriate size.
	Walk toward the front edge of the Penalty Area and measure the distance between the Penalty Mark and the top of the Penalty Area.
8	At the front edge of the Penalty Area make sure that all of the lines you can see are drawn correctly and are visible.
	Walk toward the top of the Restraining Arc and measure the distance between the Penalty Mark and the top of the Restraining Arc.
9	Make sure that the Penalty Kick Restraining Arc is drawn correctly and is visible.

Step	Description
(5)	Return to the opposite goalpost (step 5) and make sure that all of the lines you can see are drawn correctly and are visible. Walk toward the far end of the Goal Area measuring the distance between the goalpost and the edge of the Goal Area.
10	Walk toward the edge of the Penalty Area and make sure that all of the lines you can see are drawn correctly and are visible. Walk toward the far end of the Goal Area measuring the distance between the goalpost and the edge of the Goal Area.
11	Make sure that all of the lines you can see are drawn correctly and are visible. Walk toward the corner flag.
12	Check to make sure there is a corner flag (some leagues allow for a corner cone instead), it is properly placed and is the correct (at least minimum) length. Make sure the corner arc is drawn correctly, is visible and is the correct distance from the flag. Walk toward midfield
13	At midfield, make sure the sidelines are solid down both halves of the field. If there is a flag placed at midfield, make sure the flag is the appropriate minimum distance from the line. Turn left and head toward the center of the field.
14	Make sure that the center mark is clearly drawn and the appropriate size. Walk toward the far edge of the Center Circle

Step	Description
15	Make sure that the Center Circle is drawn correctly and is visible. Walk toward the center of the field and measure the distance from the Center Circle line to the center of the field
16	Walk toward the other half of the Center Circle and make sure that the Center Circle is drawn correctly and is visible. Measure the distance from the center of the field to the edge of the Center Circle line. Walk toward the far corner flag.

For steps 17 through 27, repeat the same inspections you performed for the first half you inspected.

When working as part of a three-man or four-man team, you can inspect the field together or you can split up and have each member of the team inspect a different section of the field.

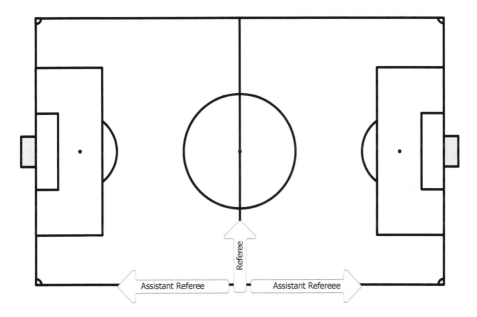

If you inspect the field as a team, you can have three or four pairs of eyes looking at the same thing. This increases the likelihood that you will catch whatever might be wrong with the field. When you inspect the field together, you have more time to talk with your team members, get to know them better and discuss in more depth how you will be managing the game together.

If you decide to split responsibilities and have each member of the team inspect a part of the field, one option is to split responsibilities as shown in "Exercise 3: Field Inspection" on page 59. With this approach, the team starts at the halfway line on one side of the field. The Referee heads across the field and covers the halfway line and the center circle while the Assistant Referees head along the outside and inspect everything along the goal line between the corner flags.

Check the Game Balls

The rules should clearly specify the minimum requirements for any ball used in a Soccer game. Requirements should include some or all of the following items:

- Weight

- Circumference

- Air Pressure

- Cover material

Make sure you know what the requirements are for the particular game you are working.

For most leagues, the Home team provides the game ball or balls. In other leagues, each team provides balls and the Referee picks the best ball or balls from the available options. Make sure you know before you get there who is supposed to provide the game balls.

Before the game, take a moment and inspect each of the balls provided by either team for use during the game. You should have equipment in your Referee Kit you can use to make sure the ball meets any requirements.

Pay special attention to any tear or cut in the outer surface of a ball. Edges or torn pieces of the ball's outer surface can cut players if sharp enough.

Do not be afraid to disallow any ball that you think does not meet the requirements or that may be dangerous to players. Even if one or more balls are unusable, you will be able to find more balls from which to choose.

Check the Roster, Player Passes and Player Equipment

Most leagues or tournaments require that players and (sometimes) coaches provide a special pass to the Referee before each game. Passes normally have a name and recent photo attached to them and are usually laminated (so they cannot be modified). You may also receive a game roster and/or game report from one or both of the coaches before the game.

 Player and Coach Passes – Make sure you understand what you are expected to do with the player and/or coach passes before you arrive at the game.

Some organizations require player passes while others require both player and coach passes. If the organization sponsoring the game requires it, you must inspect the passes before the game begins. The name and photo (if applicable) on the pass must match the name and face of the player or coach the pass is for.

Follow the guidelines provided by the organization sponsoring the game; they might want you to carefully inspect every player against the roster and player pass or merely want you to collect the roster and passes before the game, then mail the roster or game report to the league and return the passes to the coach.

Most leagues or tournaments instruct Referees to keep the pass for any player or coach ejected from a game; you would then mail the pass with the game report later.

There are two very important things to pay attention to here:

- Make sure you understand what you are expected to do with any player and coach passes before you arrive at the game.

- Be sure to return the passes to the appropriate coach after the game, making sure to keep passes for any ejected players or coaches if the league or tournament requires it.

If you leave without remembering to return the player passes or if you are supposed to keep some passes (because of any disciplinary problems) and you don't, you have created a problem for yourself. Pay attention!

It might not be a good idea to store the player and coach passes in your gear bag. If the coach wants to sneak a player in or switch someone out, it will be easy if he or she has access to your bag while you are paying attention to something else. *I always kept the player passes in my pocket or gave one team's passes to each of my Assistant Referees.*

Equipment Check Opportunity! While you are checking the player passes and/or roster, you will have an excellent opportunity to make sure that the players are wearing the correct equipment and are not wearing anything dangerous.

Check every player's equipment and don't allow anyone to play who is wearing equipment that does not comply with the rules or could possibly be a danger to a player.

Do not be afraid to disallow any player for any equipment problem. You are merely performing your job as expected and you are keeping the player's safety in mind.

Identify Uniform Conflicts

Ten to 15 minutes before the start of the game, make sure that you don't have any color conflicts with any uniforms. Make sure that the teams' colors are unique and that goalkeepers are clearly identifiable. Make sure that the officials' uniforms don't cause a conflict either.

Manage Color Conflicts Conservatively! Just because you don't think there is a conflict in colors does not mean that there isn't one.

Look at this from the viewpoints of the players and coaches. If there is ANY chance of confusion due to uniform colors, err on the side of caution and make sure that you have distinct uniform colors (according to the rules of the competition) for all participants.

Soccer players (or at least good Soccer players) play using their peripheral vision. A striker driving toward the goal with the ball will look for teammates or opponents. If you allow a goalkeeper to wear the same color as the Referee, for example, then the striker may get confused when he sees two of what he or she thinks is the defending goalkeeper.

If you have a conflict, resolve the conflict as described in the rule book that governs the contest.

Don't mess around with this; ensure before the game starts that the rules on uniforms and uniform conflicts are being followed by all participants (and that means Referees, too). Failure to take care of this before the game can cause you unnecessary stress later.

Team Instructions

It is unlikely that you will start your career as a Center Referee in a game with three or even four Referees. However, if you are the Referee in a three-man or a four-man team of officials, then you will be responsible for providing detailed instructions to your assistants. This instructing of your assistants is called the Pre-Game Conference. The materials you received during your clinic should contain information listing the type of information covered during the pre-game.

Pay careful attention to what responsibilities you should be assigning and be sure to cover everything you think you will encounter during the game. If you are not thorough and forget to cover something, then it is possible that something can come up in a game that you or your team is not prepared for and you could have trouble.

If you are an Assistant Referee or a Fourth Official for a match, you should expect the Referee to give you a thorough set of instructions during the pre-game. If he or she does not, then you should take it upon yourself to identify the things you are unsure of how to handle and ask questions of the Referee until you know for sure what you are and are not supposed to do during the game.

While any procedures guide for Referees will usually cover most options for Assistant Referees or Fourth Officials, it never hurts to make sure before the game what the Referee wants you to do. Every official has his or her special way of doing things and you will have a better experience if you make sure it is covered before the game begins.

Instructing Club Linesmen

If you are doing the game by yourself (no Assistant Referees), make sure you identify the persons who will be acting as club linesmen for you during the game. Make sure you instruct them on what you want them to do. Be sure that the instructions you give them properly reflect the duties assigned to these helpers as described in the rule book.

Don't give these helpers too much responsibility. Since they are not acting as Referees, you can't treat them as Referees. You have to give them enough responsibility so they are a help to you during the game rather than a hindrance. Again, make sure you understand what the rule book says about these helpers and give them just the right amount of responsibility.

Instruct the Ball Handlers

If you will have ball persons (someone who chases down the ball when it leaves the field) for your game, take a moment to introduce yourself to them and explain what you expect of them during the game. By giving some of your attention, you will be making them feel like an important part of the game.

Set Your Watch

The length of a game (actually the length of the periods) varies based upon age group or division. Be sure you know how long the periods are for your game and set your watch before the game begins.

Pre-hydrate

If you are working a game on a hot day or you know you have several games to do in a day, be sure to drink plenty of water *before* the game starts. Drinking water before exercise is called pre-hydrating and can help keep you fresh (both physically and mentally) throughout the game.

If you don't make sure you have enough fluids in your body before the game, you might find that you tire more quickly and have difficulty making accurate decisions during the game.

Coin Toss

Following the guidelines you received with your clinic materials, make sure to complete the coin toss early enough that everyone has time to get ready for the start of the game.

Be Prepared at Center Field! Make a checklist of everything you want to cover during the coin toss. Be sure to take at a minimum a coin, paper and pencil (or pen) with you to the coin toss.

Be sure before everyone leaves that everyone understands which team will be taking the kick-off and which team will be defending which goal. Be sure to write all of this down so you will be able to remember the information later; you will need the information to prepare for the next period.

Get Everyone on the Field

Take out the paper you used during the coin toss and review which teams will be at which end of the field and who will be taking the kick-off. Before you start the game, you have to get everyone on the field and on the correct side.

Calling Players to the Field. DO NOT blow the whistle to call the players onto the field. Walk over to each coach or team and politely notify them that you are ready to begin the game. Calling players onto the field using the whistle is rude and does not demonstrate the proper respect a Referee should have for the players.

Take the Ball with You to the Center Circle

You are going to be nervous and you are going to have many things floating around in your head as you begin your first game. Be sure to pick up one of the game balls and take it with you to the center of the field for the kick-off.

Make Sure Everything is Ready

This is it; it's time to start your first game. If you have followed the instructions in this book, you will be prepared and ready to go.

Here is a checklist you can use when checking to see if everything is ready

- Did you put sunscreen on?

- Are you properly dressed with uniform shirt and badge (if required)?

- Is your shirt tucked in? If your shorts have a draw-string, is it tied? Are your socks pulled up? Are your shoes tied?

- Do you have your watches, whistles, Yellow and Red Cards, pen, paper and other equipment?

- Is your watch set with the correct countdown time for the current game?

- Do you have the rosters from both teams (if required)?

- Do you have the player passes for all participants (if required)?

- Are there flags (or cones, if allowed) on the corners?

- Does it look like the nets are still attached to the goalposts?

- Do you have club linesmen? If so, are they ready to go? Did you remember to give them flags to use?

- Do you have Assistant Referees? If so, are they ready to go? Do they have flags? Are they in position? Have they signaled that they are ready to go?

- Are all of the players on the field? Are they on the correct side of the field?

- Do you have two goalkeepers and are they properly dressed and in position?

- Do you have any uniform conflicts?

- Are all non-playing personnel off the field?

- Do you have the game ball?

- Are you ready?

Blow the Whistle with Confidence

When it is time to start the game and you have everything ready, take a deep breath and signal to start the game. Make sure you blow the whistle with confidence and authority. *No wimpy whistles to start your game!* Show everyone that you are confident and ready.

Remember to Start Your Watches! Once you have started the game, don't forget to start the timers on both of your watches. Laugh about it and call this a stupid suggestion, but you will forget to start your watches at least once in your first season. I guarantee it.

During the Game

Remember that you are going to make mistakes — don't let it get to you when you make one. Remember all that you have learned and do the best that you can. Since it is your first game, there is going to be a lot going on and you will not be able to keep up with everything. You may have difficulty watching for the ball going out of bounds, goals being scored and players fouling each other.

Follow the procedures you were taught in the clinic and keep up with play at all times.

Be clear with your signals, use only the approved signals and make sure nobody has to guess what you mean by your signals.

Blow the whistle when you need to — and only when you need to. Be sure to blow the whistle with confidence and vary your tone so every whistle does not sound the same.

Smile. Make everyone feel as if you are having the time of your life out there on the field. It is OK to smile a little when a player does something silly; just don't laugh too loudly.

Run! Yes, I mean it — run! I know this sounds silly, but many Referees believe that since they can see the whole field from where they are (especially in small-sided games), they don't need to run much. These Referees just walk around and don't show much enthusiasm for the game. Wrong! The players are running around, the Referee should run as well. The only way you can see the most of what is happening during the game is if you are running along with the players and staying close to play. An effective Referee runs the entire time that the ball is in play. You should be at least as tired as the players at the end of the game; otherwise, you did not work hard enough.

A Referee can see so much more if he or she is in motion with the players and the ball. If you are 50 yards away, it is easy to get your view blocked by other players. If a player goes down in a tumble and you did not know what happened to him or her, it is probably because you were too far away. Run, if you are not fit enough to keep up with play, then you should not be a Referee.

Presence Lends Conviction

In my first few years as a Soccer Referee, the most common thing I heard from instructors and fellow Referees was "Presence lends conviction!" When discussing positioning and movement on the field, it was clear to me that the further a Referee was from the foul he or she was calling, the more complaints were heard from the players. If the Referee is too far away, it's easy for the players to argue that he or she couldn't have seen whatever really happened.

By being closer to play, the Referee usually sees more, even if he or she did not see everything. When a Referee is closer to the foul when it occurs, it is easier for players to feel confident in the Referee's decision.

I was working a Men's game one morning a long time ago. There was a shot on goal that the goalkeeper caught and immediately punted all the way into the other half of the field. As the ball landed, a teammate of the goalkeeper collected the ball and started driving toward the goal. At the last second, the player passed the ball forward to a player who had come up from the back to assist. I immediately blew the whistle and signaled for the offside infraction.

Fortunately for me (and them), I had started sprinting up-field as soon as the goalkeeper picked up the ball and continued to run as the play progressed toward the goal. When the pass was made, I was even with the second to the last defender, so I was in a very good position to judge the offside infraction.

When I blew the whistle, the nearby players turned to look at me. As soon as they realized I was close enough to make the call, they turned and prepared for the restart.

If I had stayed back and had not made the effort to keep up with play, they would have argued vehemently against the infringement and quite possibly could have been right. For Referees, it is hard to sell a call when you know you were not close enough to make it.

When you have a free kick, the goalkeeper has the ball in his hands for a punt or if you have a quick reversal of direction and the ball is heading down the field (often toward the other goal), the Referee has to get quickly to where play is going to be next. For a goal kick or a restart for the defenders in their own half of the field, the Referee has to position himself—if possible before the kick is taken—near where the ball is likely to end up after the kick. This is another good example of why the Referee has to run during the game, he or she has to get to where the ball is going to end up after a free kick

Try not to listen too much to the coaches and fans. Some coaches and so many fans really don't understand the game and they are just yelling to yell. Keep working hard and do the best you can. Address issues that come up and try to be consistent. Don't get too distracted by all of the yelling going on around you. Calling a foul or changing a decision just because someone yelled at you could create trouble for you later.

Rabbit Ears - Duck Feathers

Referees need to have Rabbit Ears and Duck Feathers. Rabbit Ears so they can hear everything that is going on around them and Duck Feathers so that anything said about them can flow right off of them just like water flows off a duck's back.

Don't be afraid to change your mind. The rules usually allow a Referee to change his or her decisions within certain limitations. If you have made a call, then realize that you have made a mistake, if the rules allow for you to change your decision (for example, if the ball has not been put into play yet) then go ahead and change your decision. Stop the players, point the other way and tell the players you made a mistake and you're changing your decision.

On the other hand, if you think you have seen a foul, but you are not sure, and the fans immediately start yelling about it, you may have just received confirmation that it was a foul. I am still not saying that you should call the foul because they yelled. But I am offering the possibility that if you thought it was a foul, but were not sure, the fans can give you a helping hand. Be careful how much you use this; constant application of this technique can get a Referee into a lot of trouble in the end.

As mentioned before, you will need to stay close to play during the game. As the ball nears the touch line or the goal line, you will be responsible for letting everyone know who gets to put the ball back into play. Keep track of who last touched the ball before it leaves the field over a touch line or goal line.

The cool thing is that if you are not sure who should have the restart, you can often wait a little but and see who picks up the ball. If one team picks up the ball without the other team protesting, you can often assume (if you don't know) that the correct team has the ball and is ready to go. If you don't know who is supposed to have the restart and make a decision anyway, it is hard to recover when everyone except you knows which team the ball is supposed to go to and they know you have made a mistake. When you don't know, wait a few extra seconds to see if the teams will let you know by their actions what should happen next.

Don't let pride keep you from admitting a mistake and doing what is right for the game.

Understand though, that many coaches teach their players to pick up the ball no matter who touched it last. They do this in the hope that the Referee will not know and will award the ball to the team that picked it up.

It's easy to miss a foul, and many coaches and fans will leave you alone on little ones, but to miss something as fundamental as knowing who kicked a ball out of bounds may cause you some grief. The players, fans and coaches will quickly determine that if you can't tell who touched it last then you certainly will not be able to determine anything about fouls that occur during the game.

Be sure to record (write down) every goal, Yellow Card and Red Card you have during the game. Don't restart the game until you have recorded the things you need to record. It is sometimes useful but not required to record the time of each goal and the team and player number for each injury.

The Hardest Parts of My First Games

When I started working games, I was surprised to find that I was so busy trying to see everything that was going on around me that I was unable to remember who touched the ball last before it left the field of play. I would be running along, constantly looking for fouls and offside infractions, when the ball went out of bounds I would be at a complete loss for what to do next. It was embarrassing.

What I finally did to fix this problem was to use a mental trick to help me remember who had touched the ball last. Whenever play was near the touch or goal lines and a player touched the ball, I would say the player's uniform color to myself. So, as I watched play, I would be constantly saying to myself something like "red... blue... red... red... blue... " When the ball finally went out of play, I would make sure to give the ball to the team with the color different from the last color I said to myself.

Be careful; you don't want to do something like this aloud; you don't want people thinking you don't know what you are doing.

What Will it be Like?

So, what do you think it will feel like to work your first game?

If you have played the game before, most of what happens will not be very different from what you are used to. You will just be looking at the game from a different angle. If you have not played Soccer, all of this will probably be very new to you.

As with watching a game as a fan, the Referee must also follow play and in general keep his or her eye on or near the ball. Unlike fans, though, Referees often also have to watch what's happening away from the ball. The Referee has to keep one eye out for things players do when they are not playing the ball.

During the game, you will be running along with the players, trying to stay up with play as it moves back and forth across the field.

When a team has the ball and is driving toward the goal, you will have to be sure to stay close so you can see any fouls that take away the team's chances to score a goal. If the defense recovers the ball and starts a quick-counter attack, you will have to be ready to sprint back and immediately get into position to see what happens next on the other half of the field.

On corner kicks, you will have to be in position to make sure the ball is properly played and there is no illegal interference by the defenders. As soon as the ball is kicked, you have to sprint toward the Penalty Area in order to be able to see any infractions made by either team.

As you can see from the picture I'm painting here, you will have a lot of work to do staying up with play and seeing as much as you can during the game. As you run around, trying to stay up with everything, you are also going to have responsibility for calling fouls.

Players are going to be yelling to or at each other. Parents are going to be yelling at players and at each other. Coaches are going to be yelling at the players. Someone will even be yelling at you; don't forget about Rabbit Ears and Duck Feathers. Ignore most of it.

When the ball goes over the touch line or goal line, you are going to have to be listening or looking for substitutions. Some of those yells from coaches or players are for subs, so you will have to listen to them even though you might not want to.

The ball is going to be bouncing between players, especially in the Penalty Area. You are going to be responsible for determining what is and what is not a foul. For this game, you are the deciding judge.

The funny thing is that you are going to be running around, trying to do all of the things you are supposed to be doing, getting some things right and some things wrong. Before you know it, the period will be over and it is time for the half-time break. Your watch will start beeping and you will be surprised to see that the first period is over.

What Happens if the Weather Changes?

If the weather changes during the game, you may have to make a decision about whether to continue the game, suspend the game temporarily or terminate the match.

If you see lightning or hear thunder, you should suspend the game until the storm has passed. Blow your whistle and order everyone to shelter. Monitor the weather until you no longer see lightning or hear thunder before letting anyone back onto the field. Be responsible and don't be in a hurry to get everyone back onto the field if there are still thunderstorms in the area.

If you suspend the game for weather and it is getting close to dusk, you may have to terminate the game if it gets too dark to continue play before the storms leave the area.

If the field was fine at the start of the game, but rain or snow has caused the field to become dangerous (too slippery or muddy for the players to play in a controlled manner) then you may have to terminate the game. You cannot let players play on a field if the field conditions are unsafe for them. Monitor the field conditions during a rain or snow storm and make the appropriate decision if it seems that the field conditions are causing players to lose control and get hurt.

Follow your league's rules for how to deal with terminated games. You will still have to file a report for the game and it is possible the teams will be able to finish the game later or even play the game over (depending on league rules).

Things to Do During the Half-Time Break

During the half-time break, collect your thoughts and get ready for the second half. Some of the activities you should/can do during the half-time break are:

- Be sure to start a timer or at least look at the time so you will know when the half-time break is over.

- Drink some water. If you truly worked the first half and ran around with the players then you should be in need of some fluids. Don't drink a bunch of sugary drinks or juices. Water is the best choice for you at this time.

- Make sure you have the game ball. Check to make sure it has enough pressure and that nothing has happened to the ball that can make it dangerous to use.

- Lookup anything you need to review in the rule book or your course materials. If something happened during the first half and you were not sure what to do about it, now is the time to find out so you will be prepared for the second half. You can probably not go back and fix a problem from the first half, but you can at least be prepared for the second. Be careful letting people see you look something up, but don't be afraid to look it up if you need to.

- If your uniform or shoes are dirty and you have a change or something to clean them with, take a moment to clean up.

- Communicate with the coaches regarding anything that needs clarification. Some examples of topics you could clarify are things like substitution procedures, field conditions, injuries and so on.

Things You Should Not Do During the Half-Time Break

Be careful getting into a discussion with players, coaches or fans about something that happened during the first half of the game. You don't want to get involved in any arguments or disagreements about how something should be handled. Concern yourself only with specific questions people may have about things that are not related to judgment calls you made during the game.

If people want to talk with you about something during the half-time break, you can be assured that it is probably not going to be something that you are going to want discuss. Be polite, be respectful, but be careful about what discussions you allow.

During the half-time break, I normally like to take my Referee team off to the side somewhere away from everyone else. This gives us time to talk about the first half without other people listening and it gives us time to see anyone who may be approaching us.

Do not play with the ball. Take it over to the sideline with you and put it down while you take care of your half-time business. Just because you think you're a Soccer hotshot doesn't mean that everyone wants to see you show off. Remember, you are supposed to be professional at all times.

When the Game is Over

When you have reached the end of the game, blow your whistle to signal the end and breathe a sigh of relief. You have completed your first game! There are a few steps you need to complete before you are ready to head home:

- Collect the game ball. You need to hand it back to the home coach (assuming the home team provided the ball) personally.

- Don't mingle with the players and fans. There is really no need to hang around them. It is possible they will have nice things to say to you, but that is not guaranteed.

- Retrieve your flags from the club linesmen or your Assistant Referees.

- Keep any player or coach passes you are required to keep because of any disciplinary problems you encountered during the game. Return the remaining passes to the appropriate coach. Be sure to return the passes to the coach you received them from; giving them to a player or a parent does not guarantee that they will make it back to the coach. You don't want to be responsible for losing a team's passes.

- Keep the game rosters and/or game report forms you received from the coaches. If the home coach is supposed to file the game report for you, fill out the form and give it to the coach at this time.

- Return your gear to your Referee bag and walk calmly to your car or your ride. Don't forget to take your water jug.

- As soon as you can, drink some water or one of those specialty sports drinks.

Don't react to any complaints or negative comments you receive from anyone. Either ignore the comments or say a polite "thank you" or "thank you for your comment" and move on. Nothing good is accomplished by getting into an argument except to potentially make you look bad. Act confident and professional and get out of the situation as quickly as you can.

While it seldom happens, if someone becomes aggressive and you feel threatened, don't hesitate to call out for help or dial 9-1-1. Assault of a sports official is illegal in most areas—you should be OK, but it never hurts to be prepared.

When you Get Home

Make sure you clean your uniform. Don't leave it all balled up in your Referee kit or on the floor of your closet. Get it cleaned right away so when you get ready for your next game you don't have to scurry around at the last minute trying to pull together a proper uniform.

If you worked on a dusty or muddy field, get out a scrub brush and clean your shoes. If they are muddy and/or wet, clean them well then stuff newspaper into the shoes to help them dry better from the inside (the newspaper will absorb additional moisture). The newspaper also helps them keep their shape and keeps them from shrinking. Be sure to pull the newspaper out of your shoes the next morning (8 to 12 hours later); it won't do you any good to have wet paper sitting in your shoes until your next game. If your shoes are still wet, repeat the process until they are dry on the inside and outside.

If you have to file a written report for the game, get out your notes from the game and fill out the necessary paperwork. Don't wait until the next day or the following week, get your reports done while the information from the game is still fresh in your mind. This is especially important if you had any ejections in the game and you have one or more player passes you have to mail into the league for processing.

Self-Assessment

Next, you need to think about the game, write down some notes and your plan for addressing any problems you encountered. This self-assessment will help you tune and tone your game and should become a regular part of your post-game analysis.

Get out a piece of paper and pencil. At the top of the piece of paper, write some information about you and the game. List your name, the date of the game, the date of the assessment (if different from the game date), the location, division, teams and score for the game. Write down any information you feel is important about the game.

Next, think back to the game and write down at least three things that you believe you did very well. If you thought you called some good fouls, write it down. If you felt that you dealt very professionally with the coaches, write it down. Reinforce the things you did well by writing them down and thinking about the impact they had on your game.

Now, think about the things you did not handle well. Select the top three things and write them down on the paper as well. Be sure to leave some room between each item because you are going to add some extra content to this section of the assessment later.

If you think you could have recognized fouls better, write it down. If you think you missed something that should have earned a Yellow Card or a Red Card, write it down. If you let a coach or fan get to you, write it down.

Take a moment to think about each of the items you just wrote down. Next to each one, write down the answers to the following questions:

1 - What impact did this have on the game?

2 - What can you do to make sure you deal with this issue correctly in your next game?

Think about any problems you had later that were caused by something you did or did not do. Identify steps you can take to handle this issue better the next time you are facing it.

If for example, you reacted to a coach when he or she gave you a hard time about something, think about any problems that may have caused later on in the game and decide now how you could have handled that situation better.

Seek the Advice of Experienced Refs. If stumped about how to handle certain situations, contact your Mentor or an experienced Referee you know. It never hurts to ask someone with experience how to handle things that come up during a game. Add suggestions you receive to your list of actions.

Near the bottom of the page, write "For my next game, I am going to:" followed by three or more actions you are going to take to improve your performance for the next game. These three things can be the same actions you listed in 2 above or they can be reworked into something a bit more general; something that could apply to a broader group of situations. When you are finished with your Self-Assessment, you will have your game plan already laid out and ready for your next game.

Chapter 5

You've finished your first game and hopefully you have an idea of what you will want to change for your next game. It's time to start thinking about your next game and on to the end of your first season. This section of the book contains some simple advice for the remainder of your season. Keep applying the skills you obtained in the last two sections and keep going.

Your Second Game

As you prepare for your second game, repeat the steps you took to prepare for your first game. This includes doing everything from "Practice" on page 44 all the way through the Self-Assessment in the last section.

The only addition to the routine is that you are also going to spend some time during the preparation period and just before the game focusing on the action plan that came out of your Self-Assessment for the first game.

Finishing Your First Season

Your first few games are going to be a lot of hard work. You are going to make mistakes but you are probably going to also get a lot of things right. You are going to learn new things with every game you work — in fact you never stop learning!

As you progress through your first season, you will find that you will add new things to the "Things I Did Well" section of the Self-Assessment every week and your list of things you have to work on will get shorter over time. As you gain experience, things will become easier and will not require conscious thought.

Keep doing Self-Assessments after every game, eventually you will be able to do it in your mind rather than putting it all down on paper. As long as you continue to monitor your performance and adjust your game as you go, you have a tremendous career in front of you.

Remember! Don't rush to do higher-level games. Do the games you are assigned to and advance when you feel truly comfortable. You are still learning here. There is no need for the extra stress higher divisions bring until you are ready.

Learn Something from Every Referee You See

Make an effort to learn at least one thing from every Referee you work with. You will work with a lot of different referees with many different skills, styles, approaches and levels of effectiveness. You can learn tips and techniques that you can apply to your own game but you can also learn things that you should never do.

If you see a Referee work a game and you really like something about that Referee's style, see if you can adjust your game to try to get part of that Referee's style in your game.

Be careful though and don't try to be just like that Referee! A Referee's style is the combination of the Referee's personality and the experience he or she has had doing games. You will never be able to be just like another Referee; pick and chose parts of different Referees' styles and try to make them part of your own.

Staying Organized

Keeping accurate records is very important for Soccer Referees.

When it is time to apply for an upgrade to the next level, you will need to be able to document the number of games you have worked and at what level (division, age group and so on). When you look to join the High School or Collegiate officiating ranks, you may also have to prove you have the necessary experience.

Most Referees are paid. In some cases, an official is paid in cash before the game, but in others, a check is mailed to the Referee after game reports have been processed. You should track your payments In order to make sure you receive compensation for all of your games.

In most cases, Referees are also responsible for paying taxes on any income received from officiating. Referees also spend a lot of money on uniforms and other equipment and there is mileage expense for travel to and from every game or Referee meeting. In order to be able to prepare the appropriate income tax forms (leveraging both income earned and expenses incurred), you must track everything.

Often when a player is seriously injured in a game or there are disciplinary issues that a Referee has to deal with, there is additional documentation about the game that must be maintained by the Referee. In most cases, the sheet of paper the Referee uses to track the score and any serious penalties is sufficient, but sometimes additional information must be kept. In many such cases, the Referee submits a game report with a written explanation of the injury or of the disciplinary issues.

Most Referees keep track of games, payments, expenses and reports using manual means. For computer savvy Referees, there are a few computer software programs designed to handle some or all of these tasks.

My favorite tool for keeping a Referee organized is Official's Record Keeper (ORK) from McNelly SoftWorks, LLC. This one is my favorite product mostly because I am the one who created it. I am therefore a little biased.

ORK is designed to allow a Referee to track every aspect of his or her Referee career. You can track all games, locations and expenses. For games, ORK allows you to record all the game details including sanctions, expenses, income and more. The program does not require any additional software to run and supports an unlimited number of sports. With ORK, multiple Referees working on the same computer can manage his or her own data without conflict.

ORK comes with free support, a 100-page user guide, online help and video tutorials demonstrating how to use the program. It runs on any Microsoft supported version of Microsoft Windows. You can download a free, fully functional trial version of the software from officialsrecordkeeper.com.

Other software tools for Soccer Referees include Flagbase (flagbase.com) and Referee Tracker (dataintoaction.com/referee).

Appendix A - So, Why Do It?

So, you really want to become a Soccer Referee? Are you sure? It is certainly a lot of fun, but you have to understand from the beginning that it is hard work, but very fulfilling over time. It is a great source of income for the young Referee and an incredible way to build confidence and enhance decision making ability. The trials and tribulations of everyday life are easy after you have regularly officiated in front of tens, hundreds or even thousands of temperamental fans.

Soccer has grown in the U.S. to a point that it offers a full time job for many people. Even Soccer-only businesses have popped up all over the country. When you look at any Sunday newspaper color advertising insert, you will likely find a Soccer ball before you will find an American football, baseball or basketball. Even car manufacturers have gotten on board; you will not see a television ad for any vendor's mini-van that does not include a Soccer mom opening the side door of the van to let young Soccer players in or out of the vehicle.

With this tremendous growth has come a very big problem: a dramatic shortage of officials. When I started playing, there was one organization in town offering games. Now, there are numerous leagues, lots of tournaments, traveling teams, in-house programs and indoor facilities.

 Never Enough! There is no way there could ever be enough Referees around to cover all of the games we have now or will have if the sport continues to grow. Soccer needs you to become a Referee as soon as possible.

The age of the average Soccer Referee has dropped dramatically over the years. We used to always have a roomful of adults in our clinics with an occasional child thrown in. Nowadays 80% to 90% of the students we get are teenagers (16 years old or younger). The last time I checked, the average age of the Soccer Referee in my area was about 15 years old. This has a lot to do with why the United States Soccer Federation (USSF) created the Recreational Referee Program (See "The USSF Recreational Referee" on page 100 for more information).

If you are a young adult and you are thinking of becoming a Soccer Referee, your reasons for doing it may be rather simple:

- You may be looking for a way to make some money.
- You may not be able to get another job because of your team's practice or game schedule.
- You may want to learn more about the game.
- Your club may require that a certain number of players also officiate games to help out.

If you are an adult and you are thinking of becoming a Soccer Referee, your reasons may be different:

- You may be looking for a more structured way to learn about the game your children are playing.
- Your children may be playing in a league that does not have enough officials and you want to help out when you can.
- Your children may be playing in a league that requires that every team provide at least one official.
- You may be upset about the officials you had in the past and you are thinking you can do a better job than those bozos.
- You may be bored and are looking for a new hobby.

There are even more reasons why you might want to become a Referee. Check out some of the reasons in the following sections.

Big Money

When I taught the USSF Entry Level Referee course, I always asked participants about their reasons for attending the clinic. In 9 cases out of 10, the reason students provided was "Money." There is no denying it; there is a lot of money to be made by officiating and most of it is paid in cash. At the time of this writing, the federal minimum wage for covered, nonexempt employees is about $5.85 per hour. That's less than half the price of a popular music CD at your local retailer. In comparison, the average Soccer match pays between $20 and $25 per game. Think about it; you can get about $25 an hour for running around in the sun for a few hours every weekend. That sure beats flipping burgers for four times as many hours a week to make the same money.

If you also play Soccer, it is much easier to get your officiating schedule adjusted to your team schedule than it is to get your manager at a regular job to adjust your work schedule to avoid game and practice times. When I first became an official, I worked an average of nine games per week every season. You can even officiate weekends in the spring and fall and still have that job at the pool or golf course in the summer.

Confidence

Officiating teaches confidence. If you have ever wanted the courage to ask out that cute girl at school, become an official - it will give you the confidence you need to go for it. Experienced Soccer Referees have to have a certain amount of confidence; they could not do the job if they did not.

When you start out, you may not have all the confidence you need. As you start to advance and get more experience, you will develop confidence that positively affects your life, even when you are not on the field.

Decision Making

Along with the confidence building you get from becoming a Soccer Referee, you will also get a good dose of experience with decision-making. A sports official is constantly evaluating situations and making decisions. A Soccer Referee often makes hundreds of decisions during the game. Decisions you make on the Soccer field usually affect others, often in a way that they take personally.

Decisions! Decisions! Decisions! Soccer Referees have to make accurate decisions very often and very quickly; an official has to live with most decisions once they're made.

While working a game, you can't gather your friends or your parents and ask them to help you decide about the things you have observed (or perhaps the things you have not observed). You will have to see something happen, decide what to do, tell everyone what you have decided to do and then move on.

The skills you learn here very easily carry over into everyday life. The experienced Soccer Referee does not have trouble making decisions and is therefore perceived in the workplace as a take-command, decisive person.

Knowledge of the Game

Increased knowledge of the game has to make you a better player. So many players, through a lack of real understanding of the rules, get frustrated by things that happen during the game. Players who are Referees often have a better understanding of what to expect and what they can and can't get away with during the game.

 Your Game Will Benefit! Increased knowledge of the laws of the game will help make you a better player.

Career Opportunities/Friends Everywhere

If you haven't graduated from High School or are in your early years of college, you are in the perfect position to begin a career that can help you make friends all over the country. As you build your career, you have an opportunity to work tournaments in your area, but that opportunity often expands to include invitations or assignments to work tournaments in other states, regions or even foreign countries.

There are many benefits of becoming an official. The biggest one is that you can work on your playing career at the same time as you build your officiating career—a good way to leverage talents in two areas at the same time. This officiating career can easily lead to you officiating professional games on television or even working the World Cup some day.

Fitness

As you get older, it is harder and harder to find a good reason to stay in shape.

If you are playing on one or more teams, it is easy. As you get further away from playing the game, as you build a professional career or start a family, working games helps you stay in shape and you get paid for it at the same time.

Appendix B - Referee Classifications

So, how do you become a Referee? Where do you start? This section is designed to help you understand the different types of Soccer Referees and point you toward the right clinic for your needs. If you have already taken a clinic or you have one scheduled, you can skip this section and move on.

In the United States, there are different approaches you can take as you begin your Soccer Officiating career. Your age and/or the types of games you want to work will determine which approach you take. While this information was written from a U.S. bias, the same information could easily apply to Soccer Officials in other countries as well.

The diagram on the following page illustrates the paths you can take in becoming a Soccer Referee. For Youth or Amateur Soccer, it shows a US Soccer focused approach. Some leagues are associated with the American Youth Soccer Organization (AYSO), the Referee certification path somewhat parallels US Soccer (similar materials, different course names), so you can use this diagram for either option.

The solid shapes represent Referee types/levels, while the shaded shapes represent clinics or courses that a person can take to enter the Referee ranks or advance to the next level. Solid lines between the shapes indicate transitions from a course to a licensed Referee or advancement in Referee level. The dotted lines represent transitions between one type of Referee and another.

Read the descriptions of the Referee types that follow, then come back to the diagram and look for the path that works for you. Begin at the bottom of the diagram, locate the appropriate starting point and follow the paths upward. The lines and shapes in the figure will show you what options are available to you and how much work is required to get to your ultimate goal.

What this diagram does not show is the clinics and courses that will help a Referee advance beyond the entry-level. Referees who are interested in the activities required to become a USSF State, National or FIFA Referee should review the *United States Soccer Federation Referee Administrative Handbook.*

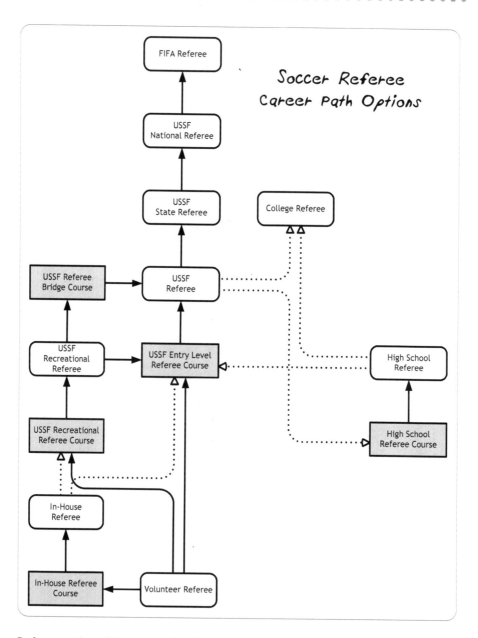

Soccer Referee
Career Path Options

Referees who wish to transfer from USSF to AYSO or AYSO to USSF can find information on the steps that must be completed in the appropriate organization's Referee handbook.

The Volunteer Referee

The Volunteer Referee is usually a parent or older sibling who steps in and works a game when there is no Referee assigned to the game or when the Referee who is assigned to the game does not show up. There is no training course or certification for this type of Referee, and I'll bet the volunteer Referee is rarely paid for his or her trouble.

Since this type of official is connected to someone playing, it is often very hard for this Referee to be truly impartial while doing the job.

Be very careful taking on the responsibility of a volunteer Referee. If someone gets hurt during the game for example, what is your liability?

The In-House Referee

Many communities offer recreational or beginner leagues. Many clubs (often as part of a bigger league) offer developmental programs often called in-house programs. These in-house programs are usually designed to offer a place for very young players to get their first experiences with the game of Soccer. Since these players are not very skilled (they are, after all, just learning the game), they typically don't require the presence of a licensed official. In many cases, one or both of the teams will provide a volunteer parent to officiate the game.

This Referee rarely wears a uniform and often does not really know much about the game of Soccer. Players identify this person as the Referee because the person is usually an adult or a much older player. So, the tallest person is usually the Referee.

Referees who work these games are usually paid, but sometimes not. It really depends on how established the program is and how much money is available to pay officials.

Many clubs have started to grow their own Referee programs. Usually an experienced parent or licensed official puts together a class and anyone who wants to work in-house games has to take the class in order to be able to work the games. In some cases, the course materials are home-grown, but in others professionally prepared material "borrowed" from some other program might be used.

An in-house trained Referee usually can't work in any games other than the ones offered by the organization. The in-house Referee is very closely tied to the organization that trained him or her and will have to go through a completely different training course in order to work games in another league or tournament.

Many of these in-house programs are affiliated with a larger organization that provides structure to the program. In many cases, these affiliated organizations provide insurance for players and officials so that if someone gets hurt, the appropriate expenses will be covered.

The USSF Recreational Referee

The USSF Recreational Referee Program is tailored to meet the specific needs of younger Referees, uses a simplified rule book (the *Simplified Laws of the Game*), requires a shorter class (half the length of the Entry Level program described below) and certifies Referees through a simpler (shorter) test. Referees who complete this program can easily upgrade later to the Entry-Level Referee program.

The program is appropriate for younger Referees of any age, but is best suited for Referees between the ages of 12 and 16. There are specific restrictions on the age level and the type of games this official can work.

A Referee who completes this program receives a badge to wear on the uniform to show completion of the certification process. Additionally, since the program is offered by USSF, any certified Referee has a certain amount of insurance coverage that protects Referees from issues that arise from injuries and other events. In today's society, where people are sued for ridiculous things, this insurance goes a long way toward protecting Referees.

The program has a yearly recertification process that requires a minimum amount of instructor-led training, a passing grade on the appropriate Referee exam and a registration fee.

The USSF Entry-Level Referee

For many years, the USSF Entry Level Referee program was the starting point for every Soccer Referee in the United States. Until the Recreational Referee Program (described in the previous section) came around, this was the only way to achieve USSF Referee certification. The program requires about 16 hours of class time, has a 100-question certification exam. It is tailored for adult Referee candidates.

In most states, you can still start with the Entry Level course, but in some, the only entry point is through the Recreational Referee program. If you are an adult Referee, the Entry-Level Referee program is the best choice for you, since you will be able to officiate any games within your skill/experience level rather than being restricted to a certain age level or division.

A Referee who completes this program receives a badge to wear on the uniform to show completion of the certification process. Additionally, since the program is offered by USSF, any certified Referee has a certain amount of insurance coverage that protects Referees from issues that arise from injuries and other events. In today's society, where people are sued for ridiculous things, this insurance goes a long way toward protecting Referees.

The program has a yearly recertification process that requires a minimum amount of instructor-led training, a passing grade on the appropriate Referee exam and a registration fee.

If you have already completed the Recreational Referee course, you can easily upgrade to Entry Level Referee by taking a special upgrade course. The upgrade course, the Referee Bridge course, requires an additional 8 hours of instruction and a passing grade on the Entry Level Referee Exam.

The High School Official

Some U.S. State High School athletic organizations offer entry-level courses for Soccer Referees. There is a national organization responsible for managing High School athletics, writing the rules, and even certifying officials: the National Federation of State High School Associations (www.nfhs.org).

If you only want to work High School games, then you can take this route to get into officiating. The High School rules are very different from other flavors of Soccer, so if you take this path, you will not be able to transition into youth or amateur Soccer without taking another Referee course.

The College Official

You can't just jump into college officiating. You must start as an amateur or high school official and get a lot of experience before you can tackle college level games.

Selecting the Best Path for You

Now that you know about the different options for becoming a Soccer Referee, which path is the correct one for you?

If you have not yet finished High School, the best options for you are to look at an in-house program or sign yourself up for a Recreational Referee course. The difference between them for you is whether you have the ability to work games outside the program (Recreational Referee) or whether you can only do games for the club that certified you (in-house Referee). Although the Recreational Referee path requires more training, the beauty of this program is that it gives you the ability to work both in-house and other games. You will probably be paid more money as a Recreational Referee and you will certainly have access to a broader range of games to work.

If your team is out of town at a tournament and you have some free time between games, or if you are at a tournament with one of your siblings, you can easily leverage your Recreational Referee certification to pick up games while you are there. The in-house Referee does not have this luxury.

If you are an adult, any of the programs would work for you. It really comes down to what you are looking to get out of being an official. If you just want to help and your children are younger, the in-house or the Entry Level Referee programs would work for you. In either case, you would be able to pick up games and help your league, club or team. If you are doing this because you love the game and want to see good games, you will want to look at the Recreational Referee program at a minimum, but the Entry Level Referee program would probably be best for you.

If you are going to stick with this for a while and you are competitive enough that how well you do matters, then you should seriously consider the Entry Level Referee program. The sky is the limit in this program; as your skills improve and you give more time to the game, you will be able to pick up higher-level games and even upgrade to higher Referee levels. Who knows; perhaps we will all watch you work World Cup games some day.

Appendix C - About Referee Clinics

To become a Soccer Referee, you will most likely need to attend a local Referee clinic. These clinics vary in duration and cost, but cover most of the information you will need to start working games. These clinics usually cover many of these topics:

- The rules (laws) of the game
- The proper markings and size of the field
- A Referee's responsibilities and obligations
- The proper Referee equipment and signals
- Game and player management
- Fitness and positioning
- Dealing with coaches and fans
- Other topics, as needed

Make sure the Referee clinic is conducted by licensed Referee instructors. Many parents or league organizers think they know enough about the game of Soccer to teach Referees, but that is very rarely the case.

Finding a Clinic

To find a Referee clinic, start by contacting your local leagues or Referee Associations. The organizations usually sponsor beginning or entry level Referee clinics before the start of every season. Because of this, start looking for clinics several months before the next season begins.

Some places to look for clinic information

- Current Referees
- Bulletin boards at local indoor sports facilities
- Local league or sports organization web sites
- Local Referee association web sites
- US Soccer State organization web sites

Some clinics require advance registration while others are open to anyone who shows up.

Many clinics run across one or two weekend days while others schedule class time across several weekday evenings. You should be able to find a clinic that fits your work or school schedule.

Most organizations charge a fee for Referee clinics.

Attending the Clinic

A lot of people show up at a clinic not really knowing what to expect.

The clinic will have a fair amount of classroom time, but there should also be some field time included. You'll therefore want to dress comfortably; dress in layers (in case it gets too hot or too cold in the classroom) and make sure your shoes will be comfortable for sitting around all day but also capable of being worn while running around a gym or an outdoor field.

You will want to bring a notebook or some paper plus a pencil and eraser or a pen. You should receive course materials during the clinic, but you will want something to take extra notes on.

Unless the clinic information indicates that lunch and/or snacks will be provided, you will want to bring some snacks, a lunch and/or money for vending machines. Don't bring or buy a lot of sugared drinks, be sure to bring only water. The sugar gives you a little kick, but when that wears off, you'll crash and will have a hard time staying awake.

If there's a fee for the clinic, be sure to bring it with you at the start.

Appendix D - Additional Reference Material

The books listed in this section provide additional information for Referees looking to become a better officials or enhance their careers.

Table 1: Books for Soccer Referees

US Soccer Laws of the Game - The U.S. standard laws of the game published by the United States Soccer Federation. It can be downloaded from the US Soccer web site at www.ussoccer.com.

US Soccer Laws of the Game Made Easy - The U.S. standard laws of the game simplified for the younger Referee, published by the United States Soccer Federation. It can be downloaded from the US Soccer web site at www.ussoccer.com.

US Soccer Advice to Referees on the Laws of the Game - Contains additional instruction for Referees on the application of the Laws of the Game. It can be downloaded from the US Soccer web site at www.ussoccer.com.

US Soccer Guide to Procedures for Referees, Assistant Referees and 4th Officials - Describes the coordinated efforts among the Referee and his Assistant Referees. It can be downloaded from the US Soccer web site at www.ussoccer.com.

Soccer Officials Guidebook for a Crew of Three Officials (Diagonal System of Control) by Carl P. Schwartz - This is US Soccer's official guidebook for Referees, covering every aspect of the Diagonal System of Control used by Referees to manage the field of play. It is an excellent study guide and reference for Referees. It can be purchased from any bookstore; refer to ISBN 978-1582080109.

FIFA Laws of the Game - The international version of the standard Laws of the Game of Soccer. This is the base Soccer rule book used by all countries. While most of the information in this book will be the same as your local version, there are sometimes minor differences that are worth knowing. This publication can be downloaded from the FIFA web site at www.fifa.com.

Table 1: Books for Soccer Referees (Continued)

FIFA Questions and Answers to the Laws of the Game - Contains questions (and the corresponding answers) for all aspects of the Laws of the Game. This is an excellent source for review questions and can help promote a better understanding of the laws of the game. When I first became a US Soccer State Referee, many of the State Referee test questions were taken from this book. It can be downloaded from the FIFA web site at www.fifa.com.

For the Good of the Game by Robert Evans and Edward Bellion. In this book, legendary US Referees Robert Evans and Edward Bellion discuss their careers and the tricks and techniques they learned that helped them become better Referees. A lot of great analysis of player personalities and gaming strategies can be found here. This book is recommended for more advanced Referees and can be purchased from any bookstore; refer to ISBN 978-1889424088.

The Art of Refereeing by Robert Evans and Edward Bellion. This appears to be an updated version of *For the Good of the Game*. This book is recommended for more advanced Referees and can be purchased from any bookstore; refer to ISBN 978-0713672114.

Referee Publications

Subscribe to any sport or Referee related publications you can locate.

- Referee Magazine (www.referee.com) contains a lot of useful information for Soccer Referees but also covers common topics affecting any sports official.

- Soccer America (www.socceramerica.com) contains a lot of useful information about the game of Soccer and other information that can be useful to Soccer Referees.

Referee Web Sites

Search around the Internet for sites containing information about Soccer officiating or generic information for any sports official. Here's a short list to get you started:

Table 2: Referee Web Site

Description	Site
American Youth Soccer Association - The AYSO is a nationwide non-profit organization that develops and delivers youth Soccer programs.	www.soccer.org
Ask a Soccer Referee - a site where Soccer Referees can ask questions related to the Laws of the Game and match situations.	www.drix.net/jim
FIFA - The official web site for the Federation of International Football Associations. This site contains copies of the international laws of the game plus additional Referee reference materials.	www.fifa.com
The Football Association - The official web site for England's governing Soccer organization.	www.thefa.com
United States Soccer Federation - This site contains downloadable Referee manuals and other publications plus Referee instructional materials.	www.ussoccer.com
National Organization of Sports Officials (NASO) - the world's largest organization for sports officials.	www.naso.org

Referee Mailing Lists

Subscribe to mailing lists that allow officials to share information and experiences with other officials. There are so many available that it would be difficult to list them all here. Google will point you to all sorts of lists.

Notes:

Official's Record Keeper (ORK) is an easy to use, affordable software tool designed specifically for sports officials. ORK manages all your referee information in one place and makes it easier for you to know where you are going, where have been, how much you have earned (including how much you're owed), how much you have spent and what happened during each of your games.

ORK helps a sports official:

- Manage a calendar of games (games, matches, meets and more)
- Track fees and payments
- Store detailed information for every contest: including partici-pants, score, sanctions and more
- Track expenses
- Track locations (fields, parks, tracks, courts)
- Associate games for each sport with specific sports organizations and/or associations

Use the power of ORK to generate reports for:

- Record keeping
- Annual registration
- Upgrade requests
- Player Disciplinary hearings
- Tax return preparation

You can even print calendars for your family or friends so everyone will know when you have to work and when you're free for other stuff!

Free Trial Version Available

Don't take our word for it, download a free, fully functional trail version of the program from www.mcnellysoftworks.com and see for yourself how the program can help you get organized like a Professional Referee.

Your Schedule at a Glance

You can view your games using the built-in calendar or you can switch to views showing game data in many useful ways. From the calendar, you can view your schedule by month, week or day. Using the dynamic data display capabilities of the program, you can slice and dice the data almost any way you want—sorting, categorizing and filtering on any value displayed in the view. Once you've displayed the data the way you want, one click sends the data to the printer.

When you finish a game, just enter the results and any other information on the game into the program. If your sport uses special sanctions to penalize participants (such as the cautions and send-offs used in Soccer), you can define the appropriate sanctions in each sport and document occurrences for every contest.

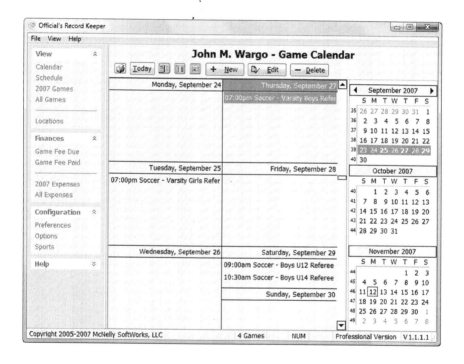

Reports

If your sport requires that you submit information about the matches
you worked for annual re-registration or requesting an officiating
level upgrade—those reports are available with a few clicks of a mouse.
When it comes time to prepare your tax return, you can use ORK to
generate the reports your accountant needs to complete the job.

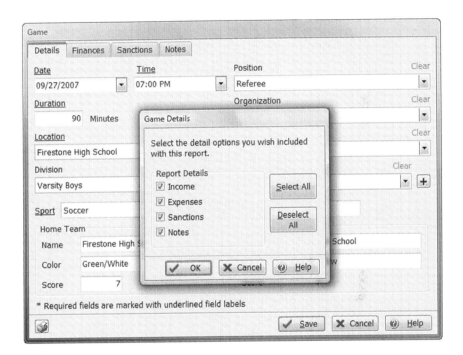

Tutorials and Documentation

ORK was designed to give you as much help as possible when you use
the program. It has a complete user guide (in Adobe Acrobat™
format), complete online help plus interactive tutorials that
demonstrate all of the features of the program. If you're using ORK
and you don't know what to do, click the nearby Help button and
you'll get all the help you need.

Officiate More Than One Sport? No Problem!

The Professional Edition of ORK gives you the ability to configure multiple sports to track your entire schedule or view schedule and information for each sport. ORK lets you to view and sort the information by sport in a variety of ways. Since the sports are defined separately, generating specific reports for each sport is a snap.

System Requirements

ORK runs on any current Microsoft supported version of Microsoft Windows™ (Windows Vista, Windows XP, Windows 2000 and Windows Millennium Edition).

Made in the USA
Lexington, KY
28 October 2013